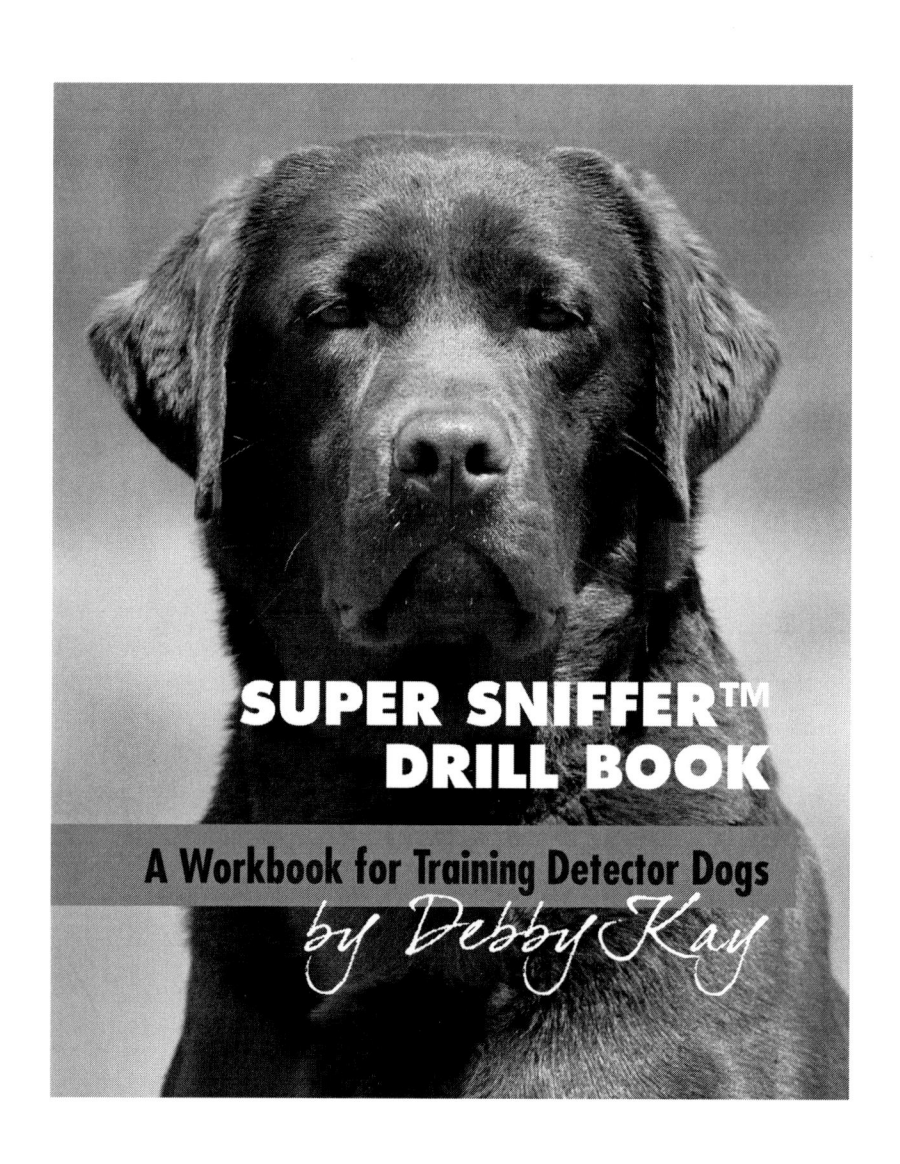

# SUPER SNIFFER™ DRILL BOOK

## A Workbook for Training Detector Dogs

*by Debby Kay*

SUPER SNIFFER™ DRILL BOOK. Copyright © 2011 by Debby Kay. All rights reserved. Printed in the United States of America. No part of this book may be used or reproduced in any manner whatsover without the written permission of the author except in the case of short quotations. For information: Coveran Publishing House.

Limits of Liability and Disclaimer of Warranty
The author and publisher shall not be liable in the event of incidental or consequential damages in connection with, or arising out of, the furnishing, performance, or use of the instructions and suggestions contained in this book.

FIRST EDITION 2011

ISBN 978-0-9837856-0-6

Library of Congress Control Number: 2011932505

Design by Nancy McKeithen

# SUPER SNIFFER™ DRILL BOOK

## A Workbook for Training Detector Dogs

### by Debby Kay

Coveran Publishing House

# DEDICATION

This book is dedicated to my late detector dog partner, Chilbrook Mandingo, a black Labrador Retriever born May 15, 1986. He had boundless energy and enthusiasm for his work that kept me motivated even when things looked bad. He had an extraordinary sense of smell that never ceased to amaze those who watched him, but mostly he had a wonderful sense of humor that always kept me laughing.

# TABLE OF CONTENTS

Introduction ............................................................................................ 9
Part I: First Steps ................................................................................. 12
    Learning the Target Odor ............................................................ 13
Part II: Basic Foundation Drills ......................................................... 22
    The Building Blocks ..................................................................... 23
        Aids in a Row Drill ................................................................ 24
        Aids in Cans Drill .................................................................. 26
        The Training Wheel Drill ...................................................... 28
        Odor Discrimination Drill .................................................... 32
        Follow My Hand Drill ........................................................... 36
        Response Improvement Drill ................................................ 38
Part III: Advanced Work ..................................................................... 40
    Making The Transition ................................................................. 41
        Casting Drill—Outside ......................................................... 42
        Buried Drill for Cadaver Dogs ............................................. 46
        Buried Drums and Tanks Drill ............................................ 48
        Box Shuffle Drill .................................................................... 50

|    |    |
|---|---|
| Follow the Seams Drill—Suitcases | 54 |
| Follow the Seams Drill—Freight | 58 |
| Follow the Seam Drill—Vehicles | 60 |
| Room Search Drill | 66 |
| Follow the Seam Drill—Windows | 70 |
| Follow the Seam Drill—Doors | 72 |

## Part IV: Practical Matters ............76
### Safety and First Aid ............ 77
- Cuts and Bleeding ............ 78
- Insects and Parasites ............ 78
- Heat Stroke and Hypothermia ............ 78
- Poisons ............ 79
- Choking ............ 80

## Appendix ............ 82
- Resources ............ 83
- About the Author ............ 85

## Index ............ 89

# INTRODUCTION

In the 39 years I have been active in dog training, I have seen a lot of changes in training philosophies and methodologies, some bad but most very good. The most significant trend change in training philosophies has come with the recent wave of positive reinforcement trainers. There is nothing new about these methods; they are only repackaged versions of works written decades earlier. What is different is these new positive methods are more widespread and generally accepted today. People are beginning to realize on a broader level that you do not have to physically dominate or control a dog in order to teach him the lessons of what you need them to do. In fact, dogs learn better when there is little to no negative reinforcement used, and learn the best when they can figure out the desired response on their own. I have found one of the constant truths about dogs is that they always learn and retain what they learn when they figure something out on their own.

With the idea of letting the dog figure out what to do to get the reward, the exercises in this book are set up to limit his choices and direct him at the same time as we wish. The dog still calls the shots in his own mind, but you get the desired response.

I did not want to limit this book to professional security and law enforcement personnel. Certainly most of my professional career has been working with this group, which comprises the largest number of users of detector dogs. I have always believed people should enjoy their dogs by exploring the many possible activities that can be done with them. Scent work is one of those activities that I consider the most fun, and all dogs can learn to perform it at varying capacities. I have included tips and suggestions throughout the book for amateur trainers as well as pet owners who are interested in teaching their dogs to find everything from truffles, buried plastic and chrysalis to any number of other items. Doctors have used dogs in therapy work for many decades but they are now learning how dogs further educated can assist in new realms of scent work. Dogs are used successfully today to detect seizures, schizophrenia, and even some forms of cancer. Dogs are incredibly adept at sensing the chemical changes associated with many disease states. The possibilities are nearly endless.

I have had the opportunity over the past three decades to train dogs to do many unique and interesting jobs. I am sure there are jobs for detector dogs I have not done or thought of. I hope in reading and learning about this methodology, you will be encouraged to explore new avenues of scent work with your dogs. I also hope you will find, as I have, that you do not have to limit detector training to the more commonly associated breeds; rather, there is something that all dogs of any breed can find to do in detector work. One of my most brilliant detector dogs was a tiny Chihuahua I owned many years ago, a most unlikely detector dog if there was one. I encourage you to keep an open mind when you think about what you want to train your dog to find. Do not go with preconceived, negative or limiting thoughts. I refer to these as killer phrases, and they have no place in my program and should not in yours. Leave behind your prejudices for breed preference, sex, discrimination and pedigree also. The notion that foreign-bred dogs perform better than domestic-bred dogs, purebred verses crossbred or mixed bred has no place in my book. They all end up doing a great job when they finish the program outlined here.

All references to the dogs are in male gender throughout the book. I in no way wish to indicate that males are preferred over females; both make great detector dogs. Another convention I use throughout is the word "repetition." In this context, it means the act of performing the drill. Each time you run through a drill it is one repetition. This book has evolved from my Super Sniffer™ workshops and is not meant as a stand-alone book on detector dog training. I am assuming the reader has either attended my workshop or graduated from some type of detector dog training course. This assumption is important because I do not explain many of the introductory steps of the exercises. I also assume you know how to make up your training aids and know the proper protocol for handling them. This book assumes you are using a food reward-based training program with a passive sit response. You can still find value with the exercises, especially the troubleshooting part, if you are using a different reward system but you will have to make your own adaptation where necessary. I ended the book with a section on safety and cannot stress this enough for any dog owner, trainer or handler. Your and your companion's safety should always be paramount. Your partner depends on you so please take the time to become familiar with safety and first aid.

I wish you as many memorable hours with your partner as I have had over the years with mine. Detector work is some of the most gratifying work you will ever do with your canine friend.

Debby Kay
Harpers Ferry, West Virginia

# PART I:
# FIRST STEPS

# LEARNING THE TARGET ODOR

Introduction to the target odor is the single most important step in the entire training process and I cannot stress enough that you should not cut any corners with this step, or try to cheat in any way. As trainers, we have a tendency to try to speed things along. For some, the fact that they can do it faster then the next person seems to make them feel as though they have done it better. WRONG! Speed is not the measure of success during this introductory stage of training.

Each session is staged carefully for success and should be attempted only when you are in a positive frame of mind. This part of the program is for many trainers the most boring part and as a result, they approach it with a less than exuberant outlook. The trainer's frame of mind is very important during this initial stage. Your dog does not have a clue what you are expecting from him and if you are less than positive, you will add to his confusion. You want him to love his work and you need to set the example.

Your training area for these first two weeks of introduction to the odor should be a place not used for any other purpose during this time. It can be as small as 8 feet x 8 feet but should not be so large that the dog has too much open space to explore or distract him. There should be nothing in the area. Ideally, I prefer a place indoors with no windows. The room should never have contained anything remotely related to the target odor you are training the dog to find. For example, do not use a room where fertilizer was stored if you are training an explosives dog. Likewise, do not use a room where vinegar was stored if you are training a narcotics detec-

*ABOVE: Sniffer tins come in various sizes. This one fits nicely in the palm of the hand. Whatever container you use, it should be new and of non-reactive, unbreakable material. BELOW: It's important to feed a reward near the tin.*

tion dog. You want the room to be as neutral as possible in regard to odor. If it was recently cleaned let it air out for several weeks before using it for detector training.

For the first week's sessions you will need only your first target odor. If you are training an explosive detection dog, this will be smokeless black powder, for the narcotic dog marijuana, and for the accelerant dog diluted gasoline. For other types of detectors, there is usually only one odor and that is the one you use. For example, if you are training a detector for natural gas pipeline leaks you will be training only on mercaptoacetic acid. The same single odor idea is true for the biological detectors and even to some extent the cadaver dogs.

## Helping Your Dog Put the Pieces Together

Bring your hungry dog, your one training aid, and some of your food treats into the room. Your dog should not be on a leash during this part of the training. In fact, I want to emphasize that you should in no way direct the dog—not with a leash or even your voice—during this part of the training. This is a time of discovery for your dog, of what works and what does not. Let him learn on his own; keep your mouth shut. Let the dog loose in the room and close the door. Go to the middle of the room, hold out the aid in the palm of your hand and say nothing. It will depend on the dog how long before he will come over and sniff the aid but he will eventually. Exactly at the moment the dog sniffs the aid have a small bit of food in the appropriate hand and bring it up until your food hand is on top of the aid. Open your hand without moving it and expose the food for the dog to eat. When the dog takes it, praise him enthusiastically. Repeat this until all your food is gone. If you are feeding dry food and have a medium to large dog, this should be between 75–100 reward repetitions. You want to do as many as you can. This is not always easy with small dogs but don't worry—even small dogs get the idea quickly that this is how they get good, and if they're hungry they will play the game.

You will notice a couple of things in this first week. First, we are not yet putting a command to this behavior. We are totally letting the dog set the pace in the exercise. I believe dogs always learn best when they learn on their own. Another thing you will see is that by the end of the week this session will take far less time. Most dogs will hardly leave the training aid by the end of the first week. They will first sit on or stand over the aid and keep sniffing the aid to get another piece of food. That is okay. We are building a memory here that will be the foundation of the work. You can pivot around to make the dog move or go to a different spot in the room to get him to move. Just be sure you are giving him food only when he actually sniffs the aid. Remember, dogs learn from repetition and we want to have as many repetitions as we can for them to learn.

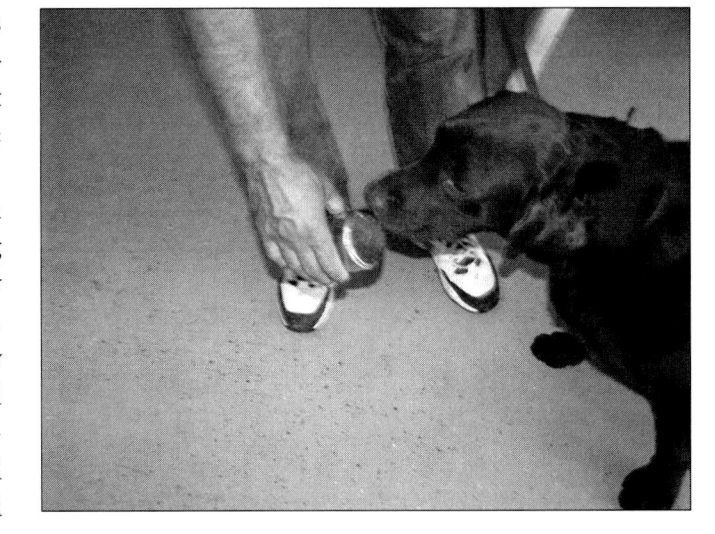

Some key points to remember when executing this part of the training are to always keep your hand with the food on the top of the training, then open it for the dog to take the food. Try to think of it like the dog does: "If I smell this odor the food appears on it. Therefore, I want to stay close to the source of the odor." The usefulness of this pattern of the dog sniffing the target odor and staying right there will become more apparent as we proceed. But suffice to say here, it is to assure you of great accuracy in your future field work. Another point is your food should appear almost simultaneously with the dog's action of sniffing the training aid. Learn to watch your dog carefully to be sure he is sniffing the aid and not just putting his nose on top of it. You will pay dearly for mistakes made here when you try to move later to more advanced work. So pay attention to the slightest detail of every move.

For the toys and small breeds almost toy size, I recommend training at this stage of the game on top of a table with a non-skid mat. That way you can see for sure that the dog is sniffing and give the reward at the appropriate time.

**PRO TiP**

When a dog sniffs, his nostrils flare at the sides. Watch for this and you will be sure you are rewarding him when he sniffs.

If you are working the toys on the table the first three weeks, you should have no problem moving to the floor. If there is some hesitation from the dog, you may need to do a few more repetitions on the table, then try a few on the floor until the dog understands we are now moving on and doing it on the floor. All this effort can be avoided by working on the floor from the beginning. The choice is yours, but as I said, I have had an easier time working toys on a large table first.

You should record your session in your notebook while it is fresh in your mind. Make sure your dog has access to fresh water after the sessions. I always engage in my dog's favorite activity with him after a session. For most of the working breeds, this is a good game of fetch the ball. For others a good romp and a vigorous brushing seem to bring a smile to their faces. Whatever your dog likes, associate that thing with this training so he has something to look forward to at the end of the sessions. Over the next weeks of training, it will help to build the repertoire you will need in your partner for the more difficult nose work.

One of the more common behaviors I have seen with dogs first starting this program is ignoring the aid. It is difficult for people to be patient enough with a dog that is in charge of the exercise but patience is what you need these first few days. A dog may first go and lay down and totally ignore you. If you wait 15 minutes and he is still ignoring you, then I would put him away, without a single word from you, and try later. Usually after two repeats of this drill the dog will start to get hungry and curious and will at the very least nose the training aid. If that is the only thing you can get a stubborn dog to do, then reward it, not with a big flourish of accolades, just a nice "good dog."

If you are working with a "hold out" type dog, then show him you have the food. Hold the aid where he can see it. He should go to it and then you reward him, with lots of verbal praise to encourage him to repeat the action. If after showing him the food he still won't sniff the tin, tap it gently with your finger and see if he will look at it. It may just be that the dog will not put his nose right next to the aid in the beginning in spite of your best efforts. It this is the case, you may have to shape the behavior a little to get the proper response. Shaping behavior is simply incrementally getting the dog to go from one pattern to another pattern of behavior through positive reinforcement. For those familiar with the clicker training methods first introduced by Leon Whitney DVM[1] in the early 1960s, you know that there may be a few more steps in the beginning. When the light bulb goes off eventually in the dog's head the rest of the training will be downhill. I see nothing wrong in taking the extra time if you are training your companion to find truffles or whatever, but for a professional this should be a clue that you may not have a dog that will hold up under the pressure of future fieldwork. It is true that any dog can be taught to detect and alert to a particular odor using this method, however, the degree to which they perform will vary. Professionals need reliable working partners and too many difficulties at this stage will only lead to more complex problems down the road. So be alert that if you continue to have problems at these early stages you should consider using another dog for professional work.

When you are shaping the dog's behavior at this stage you are rewarding the dog at first for being close to the aid until he is comfortable getting close to it. When the dog is working well close to the aid, your next step is to withhold the reward. He will offer the behavior and get a little frustrated that you are not rewarding him and will try to do something else to get you to reward him. If he moves just a wee bit closer to the aid, offer a small piece of the food reward and an encouraging "yes, good dog!" verbal praise. It usually does not take long for a normal dog to figure out that you are looking for some different type of behavior. He will start to offer more and different behaviors and what you need to do at this point is be patient and try to encourage the behavior of putting his nose

---

[1] *The Natural Method of Dog Training*, M. Evans & Co. New York, NY, ©1963, p. 33.

**PRO TiP**

Watch your body language when you are working to be sure you are not giving the dog the wrong impression. Often your body language can be threatening to your dog even though your voice and other actions may be encouraging.

An excellent discussion on drives and body language influencing the dog's behavior is presented by Jack and Wendy Volhard in their Motivational Method 1994. See their website at www.volhard.com.

on the aid and not some of the others he may offer. Just as soon as he puts his nose on the aid, whether by accident or deliberately, give him a huge food reward, carry on, and fuss verbally over what a smart and wonderful dog he is. End the session on this positive note. At this point, I like to have the dog rest for maybe 30 minutes in his crate so he can think about the action that just got them the big payoff and seemed to make you the happiest.

When offering the big reward, some people use a special treat, such as a favorite extra large dog biscuit or a chunk of sausage or cheese, while others just feed a big handful of food. Whatever you do, make sure you are feeding it on top of the training aid. This is also true when you are shaping the behavior and he is still not putting his nose on the container to sniff. You should still reward this behavior by placing your hand on the top of the aid and opening it, exposing the food inside. The dog will be noting that he always is getting the food at the source of the odor even though it may take him a few trials longer to realize that he has to sniff here first.

You can begin to introduce the command "find it" toward the end of this initial introduction to the target odor. In fact you can begin to move around the room and hold the target odor in different places, including on the floor, or against the wall, just to get the dog used to seeing it in different places.

These first weeks go slowly and are quite boring from the trainer's standpoint. However, the change that occurs as you continue the training using this method is exponential and quite dramatic. As trainers we owe it to the dog to give him every chance to succeed and grasp the basic concept we are teaching at this point—when you sniff this particular odor you get a reward. Not all dogs learn at the same rate and much depends on their backgrounds and how much training they have had previously. Another key factor is your relationship with the dog. Obviously, if this is your primary companion and you have been doing other training with him, things will go faster and he will learn the lessons in leaps and bounds. Only you can judge the quality of the dog's work and whether that suits your purposes, but I must stress that while this part is boring to you it is very critical to your dog's education, so please be patient and maintain a high level of enthusiasm throughout.

The one thing you most definitely want to avoid is putting the dog in a stressful situation or causing him to have additional stress from confusion. Dogs under stress will learn behaviors that are very difficult to overcome. Temple Grandin in her excellent book *Animals in Translation*[2] discusses that extinction of a behavior does not erase the behavior from the brain, rather a new learning that is contrary to the old learning takes place. The learning that takes place under the stress will still be in the dog's emotional memory. What I have tried to set up in the program outlined here is avoiding as much stress on the dog as possible so his only learning experiences (hence, memories) are the ones we are looking for. Losing your patience and trying to force the dog to smell are two of the more common problems I see with trainers that cause undue stress for the dogs.

I am often asked, more by professionals than companion dog trainers, how I know if a slow learner is going to be a bad worker or not. My answer is experience in having trained literally hundreds of dogs with this method. Mostly, I look for how willing the dog is to work for something. If the dog is really trying but just doesn't understand the exercise, then that is a problem we can work out. If the dog is not trying at all no matter whether or not he learns the lessons, he will not be a good working partner. I remember in one of my classes a particular yellow Labrador named Jenny who started out by refusing to work. I observed the trainer trying everything correctly to get her to work and she would not budge. What I determined based on her reactions was that she had been punished before for sniffing things, so with great patience I worked with her for about an hour and eventually convinced her that in this new life it was perfectly okay to sniff things. Once we got over that hurdle, she turned out to be a stellar detection dog.

Obviously, from this example it is important to know about the background of the dog you are working since it plays a big factor in how well you will succeed. Unfortunately, dog behaviors are so often so meticulously controlled by people that when dogs are allowed to do something on their own they are almost afraid to act. The most extreme cases are the ones in which I have seen the most dramatic effect after going through this training method. These personality types seem to gain a new sense of self-confidence not observed prior to the training. There are equally dramatic results for dogs that have been under constant pressure from more rigorous and compulsive training methods. After the compulsive trained

---

[2] *Animals in Translation*, Temple Grandin and Catharine Johnson, Harcourt Inc., New York, NY, ©2005.

dogs learn that they get to make some decisions you almost see the tension melt from their faces. I think this is why the program has been so successful with such a wide array of dogs: It allows the dogs to reach the conclusion that their work is okay without the pressure and tension that many times comes from other methods.

*When a team works smoothly together, there is trust and no stress for either dog or handler.*

# PART II:
# BASIC FOUNDATION DRILLS

# THE BUILDING BLOCKS

The remainder of the book is a series of drills presented as Basic and Advanced based on the way the Super Sniffer™ courses are taught; hence, many things are assumed and not explained. If you are handling a dog that is already certified and having trouble with one particular type of search, you will find an equivalent drill with a troubleshooting section and a Pro Tip to help you work through the problem. For students of the Super Sniffer™ courses, following the order of the drills that apply to what you are training your dog for will be in keeping with my building block theme of teaching the dogs.

# AIDS IN A ROW DRILL

**Purpose of the Drill**

This is a very basic drill to get the dog started on doing systematic searches. Most dogs master this in two–three sessions and are ready to move on.

**Dog's Proficiency**

Must know the target odor but does not need to have a solid alert or sit response, as this can be taught during this drill.

**Equipment/Training Area Needed**

A quantity of small handheld tins, one of which is positive and the others are blank  This is best done inside but can also be done outside on a sidewalk, parking lot or short grass. If you are working on pavement, be aware of the temperature of the pavement from the heat of the day and do not ask the dog to work on hot pavement.

**Steps in Executing**

Have all your blank tins in a row spaced about 3 feet apart. At one end have your dog do several "finds" on the positive tin while it is in your hand. After several repetitions, have your dog stay or have someone hold him while you take the positive in your hand and place it at the end of the line opposite from your dog. Get your dog and start working the line, starting with the first blank on the end opposite the positive you just placed. You will be walking backward, leash in left hand and right hand sweeping over the top of the tins, palm upward. Tell your dog to "find it" or "seek" or whatever your search cue word or phrase is while you walk.

*Photo right: To distinguish the tin with the target odor, punch the holes in a different pattern from the other tins.*

The first time most dogs do this, they will want to go to the end where they saw you put the positive. If your dog wants to breeze by you, spin around to slow him down and start over, telling him to sniff each tin. That is the whole point here. We want to start early in the training to establish that your role is to direct the search; his role is to sniff where you direct and alert when he gets to the target. He does not make the decision of skipping things and get away with it. Correct that habit now at this early step and you eliminate a lot of headaches later on in his training. Once you have convinced him to slow down and sniff each one, you can begin on subsequent times to have someone move the positive for you while you move the dog away from the tins. Keep him guessing and everyone once in a while make all the tins in the line blanks.

The biggest problems, which I already mentioned, are the dog going too fast and the dog going to where he saw the positive put. This is a nose exercise, not a visual one, and the dog must learn early on that in detector work he rely only on his nose—not your eyes—to find the positive training aids. This will ensure the quality of your work as you move to real world work situations.

### PRO TiP

To slow down the fast dog, spin around and re-target the tin, commanding "find it" or whatever your cue word or phrase is to sniff. Repeat if needed until he understands he must check all the tins with his nose.

## Troubleshooting

## AIDS IN CANS DRILL

**Purpose of the Drill** — This drill prepares the dog for the subsequent drills of cans in cinder block configurations and wheel work.

**Dog's Proficiency** — A dog needs to know his target odor.

**Equipment/Training Area Needed** — This is best taught indoors. You will need at least six to eight pint-size paint cans, the same amount of gallon-size paint cans and one positive handheld training tin.

**Steps in Executing** — You will need to set up two rows of cans, one of pints and one of the gallon-size paint cans or something similar. The cans should be space about 3 feet apart in the row and the rows should be about 6 feet apart. What we are going to do is get the dog use to working with different size and shape objects. This is a very simple drill do not try to make it more complicated. For some dogs you will only need to do this once and they are ready to move on. For others who learn differently or more slowly this extra step offers them the opportunity to process the information. It might seem silly and trivial to some people but I have seen where with certain dogs it makes a difference between them succeeding or not. So use this as needed, reading your dog to see if they are comfortable with and understand the exercise of sniff what is presented to them and sitting when they find the target odor regardless of the size or shape of things.

When you pick up the target odor training aid have your dog sniff it in your hand and give a small reward. Have him watch you put it in a pint sized container and put the lid on. Turn around with your dog and approach the can giving your cue word to "find it." Reward if he sniffs and alerts as he should. If he does not sniff as he should try again but approach from a different angle. If the dog is not picking up that this is still the target odor he should alert on, even though it is in a new place, you may have to pull the target odor from the can and hold it over top of the can for one or two repetitions then place it in the can so he can make the connection. Once you have him working that one can well enough, approach the whole line of cans, walking backwards, presenting the cans with your right hand sweeping over the can tops open palm up position. You may in the beginning have to repeat your search cue word such as "find it" over each can to get him to sniff each; but many dogs will naturally sniff everything that crosses their path.

When the dog is comfortable with the pint-size cans, take up the positive from that line and place it in one of the gallon-size cans that has an "X" scratched on the surface (see photo right). Have a person who has not touched the target odor place all the other pint-size cans inside the remaining gallon cans. Repeat the drill with these cans now until the dog understands that it does not matter what you ask him to search his job is to sniff. The fact that everything looks alike to the dog eliminates the possibility that he is using visual cues to help him find the target odor. Be sure to move the target odor can around in the line up so it is not in the same place all the time.

Some dogs will hesitate at each new step and it is these dogs that will need to stay on this drill until they are very comfortable. Make the drill simpler if your dog is having trouble at first. If he won't do a row of cans make it just two at first, then three then five then seven. At any point he feels insecure or does not look like he is getting it, take away one can. Add the can back in once you get three good repetitions.

**PRO TiP**

Make sure a different person handles the blank cans to avoid any cross-contamination from the hands. If you are worried your dog might be alerting on your scent, you can have two different people help you, one handling the target odor and one handling the blanks. This is good test to be sure the dog understands it is the target odor, not your scent, that he is alerting to.

## Troubleshooting

# THE TRAINING WHEEL DRILL

**Purpose of the Drill**

The idea of the wheel is simply to give your dog more opportunities to find his target odor. You will see that it also gives you an opportunity to work on any false alerts with distracting odors. By working on the wheel, you are also creating something in the dog's memory that allows you to add new odors easily. When a new odor is put on the wheel and there is nothing else on the wheel but that odor, most dogs will sit and see if you will reward them. If you work the wheel correctly, I assure you it will not take many rounds of the wheel for the new odor to be added to your dog's lists of things he is rewarded for.

**Dog's Proficiency**

Your dog should be working with the target odor in a large metal can.

**Equipment/Training Area Needed**

Training wheel, several new, clean cans such as paint cans, small training aids—some made up with the target odor and some with distracting odors.

**Steps in Executing**

The scent wheel is a very simple device that is easy to make and even easier to use. The "wheel" consists of two eight-foot arms at right angles to each other at their midway mark. These are mounted in such a fashion that the unit can be rotated in either direction. A sample container identical to the cans you have been using in the previous exercises is attached to each of the four arms (see photos on the next page). Material composition can be anything from wood to stainless steel. I have seen many variations of this design that have included some very elaborate stands, arms and attachment setups for the cans. You are limited only by your resources and imagination. When all is said and done, however, the plain wheel composed of two 2x4's with a paint can screwed to the end of each of the four arms and sitting on a small turnstile is all you really need. The cans and the ability to turn are the keys to consider on the scent wheel. The cans must be clean and free of contamination, so you must have an easy way to change them out.

Any other part of your wheel setup is for the handler's comfort. This is particularly true when considering height. I prefer 12 inches from the ground when I am training medium to large dogs. At this height, I do not have to bend over as far. The height has nothing to do with the training of the dog. If you are working smaller dogs, you have to adjust the size of your containers and the wheel accordingly. I have heard concern from people using the wheel that the dogs will learn to search only as far from the ground as the wheel is high, and that they have to alternate the height of every other can or every other wheel in order to avoid that from happening. I can assure you the dogs are not learning anything about height while searching the wheel for their target odor. The program has plenty of exercises built into it to avoid anything like that happening. The purpose of the wheel is to give your dog many additional discrimination exercises without you having to shift cans around. It makes your job easier and allows you to expose the dog to many different distracting odors in the other three cans on the wheel.

You should not try to add more arms to the wheel or try to make it longer or larger then it is shown here as you run the risk of cross contamination. We get around this problem by using multiple wheels which I discuss on the next page. You also do not want to go beyond the symmetry of four. Why this matters is more apparent when you think about the visual we are creating for the dog. With all things equal, everything looks the same as the dog approaches the wheel. We are forcing a dog in this situation to use his nose since we have taken away all the visual cues.

The holding containers mounted on the arms of the wheel need to be changed or cleaned at least weekly if you are training a few dogs or more frequently if you are training more dogs. You never use a wheel that had been set up for explosives later in the same day for working drug dogs unless you have changed out the "positive" can. The distracting odors can remain, as they should not be a problem. If you have the resources and space to store containers,

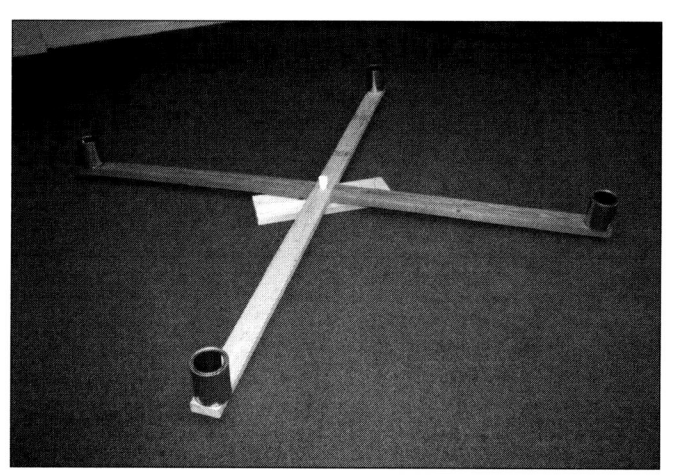

*The wheel in the top photo is less portable but at 12 inches high is comfortable for the handler. The wheel in the bottom photo is the most simple design.*

it is nice to use disposable containers such as new gallon paint cans.

The metal of the paint cans does not seem to interfere with any of the odors for anything I have trained dogs to find. Plastic, such as PVC, does seem to absorb odors and I have actually seen dogs trained with their target odor in PVC alert to PVC alone when tested. I would avoid all plastics for any of your containers. For those who do not have the resources to have disposable containers for the wheels, stainless steel is an acceptable material that is easily washed and reused. These containers can be purchased from restaurant suppliers or sometimes found in better cooking retail outlets for a reasonable price. I make sure I have two sets for each wheel I have so I can rotate them from week to week, allowing enough airing time between uses.

The setup of the wheel is simple. One can is the "positive" in which you will place your training aid with the target odor. The other cans will contain training aids made up of distracting odors. For explosive dogs that learn several types of explosives, I might use as many as 10 wheels during a training session. They are all set up together in one area. As the dog and I finish going around one wheel, we move to the next and thus make our rounds many times through all the wheels until all the food is gone.

In addition to the many repetitions you get with the wheel, this is also a good place to master your leash handling and timing. Dogs will pay attention to the minutest of details in your movement. You do not want to cue your dog with your left hand reaching in and getting food as you approach the positive can on the wheel; if you do, your dog will pick up on this and sit before sniffing. If you cannot see such details in yourself, have someone else watch you and point out any cues that might be tipping the dog off and keeping him from doing his part of the job.

When you work the dog on the wheel, you are always moving backward and presenting each can with your right hand; the leash is held loosely in the left hand. You keep moving around the wheel at a steady pace until the dog sits. When he does, you reward him by placing your hand on the training aid inside the can and letting the dog take the treats from there. You should be as close to source as you can get. If your dog has a big head, snout or is really rough, you can just lay your hand across the top of the can.

The wheel work is where you get all your repetitions in, and for dogs learning a new odor the more repetitions the better. It is also the place where you can work on getting a solid sit. After the dog has worked on the wheel for a few days, you can start to target the next can when the dog alerts. What this means is you simply continue to walk to the next can after your dog sits at the positive can, you present it with your hand and if your dog is confident at this point he will continue to sit at the positive can. The first time he does this, make sure he gets extra food and loads of praise to show this is exactly what you want him to do. From this first step, you gradually build up until you have a dog who will sit at the positive even if you tug on the leash.

If you prepared your dog properly with the Aids In Cans drill, then you should not see any trouble with the dog working on the wheel. If he is hesitant to work the wheel, work longer on the previous drill and then come back to the wheel. It may help to have the row of cans set up next to the wheel until he feels okay working on it and around it. Some dogs are sensitive to movement so just be aware of this and turn your dog away from the wheel before gently bumping it with your foot to change the can positions. If your dog starts to not sniff the cans, you are either working him too fast, not targeting each one with your hand, or rewarding the dog at his position rather than having your hand with the food over the top of the can.

If your dog will not sit on the positive in the wheel, set up a few large cans (identical to the ones on the wheel) on the floor leading up to the wheel. What you have is a row of cans on the floor with the one on the wheel being the last one in the row. It should not take more than once or twice before the reluctant dog will be sniffing cans on the wheel.

## PRO TiP

If you are going anywhere on a real search and it is close to your dog's meal time, you may want to work the dog on the wheel first, feeding a portion of his meal while doing so. It will take the edge off and he will search better for you.

## Troubleshooting

# ODOR DISCRIMINATION DRILL

This is a basic drill to teach the dog to distinguish the target odor from distracting odors.

**Dog Proficiency** — The dog should know the target odor and should sit when it is located.

**Equipment/Training Area Needed** — Scent wheel, small metal containers and several dozen clean large metal containers such as new gallon paint cans for attachment to the scent wheel.

Several dozen different items, such a small cloth bag of herbs, soap, stick of deodorant, small sample of coffee grounds, sample of dog and or cat food, and anything else your dog might be fond of or have false alerted on a previous search or practice session. This exercise can also be conducted using cinder blocks on the ground in a row or circle arrangement. If the blocks are used, a new quart paint can will fit into the hole of the block nicely; the smaller tin can then go inside the quart can.

**Steps in Executing** — When you introduce this stage of training to your dog, depending on the dog, you may want to start on the ground with a container identical to the one on the wheel. For the first 25 or so repetitions, you will be using just the one container with the target training aid inside it. Start the first repetition though by holding the target odor aid in your hand over the top of the larger container. Repeat two to five times of "find it," reward, praise. Have your dog's attention, place the aid in the container and tell him to "find it." When he will reliably go into the can to sniff the aid, you are ready to move on. Be aware you should still be feeding on top of the training aid; in other words, your hand is in the container when you open it. If you have a large-headed breed of dog that cannot fit his head into the can, then do the next best thing and feed at the top of the container opening. Once the dog will go to the can with the aid in it and there is no hesitation, set up the same situation on the wheel. To begin, have only one target odor aid on the wheel until your dog feels comfortable working on the wheel. Some dogs will take to it right away and never hesitate one bit. Others I have observed will hesitate at first but if taken slowly through all the steps will work the wheel just fine in due time. Work this drill for several days with just the one can on the wheel being positive before adding in distractions.

There are several things you can do with this drill to set up multiple learning experiences. One of my favorites, if you have the space, is to make a row of cinder blocks on the ground in either a straight line or an angled one. Set up the wheel in relation to the blocks in such a way that you can smoothly continue your search pattern from the blocks to the wheel. If you have two wheels, you can have a wheel on either side of the blocks; if you have only one wheel, you can put a few blocks on one side of the wheel and more on the other side. The point here is to present a new picture to the dog. We are teaching him many secondary things with the drill in addition to scent discrimination. Part of what we are always working on is to develop a natural flow and rhythm to the search; also, we want the dog to learn to trust his nose and changing the search picture is one sure way to do this.

Now that the dog is working comfortably around the row of blocks and on the wheel, you can start to add in distracting odors. I would not start with anything too pungent; salt, soap, dryer sheets and gum might be a set to use in the beginning. Enough of the distracting odor is placed in the small tins with holes punched on the top just like the positive one and these are placed in the remaining three containers on the wheel. Mark your positive by scratching an X on the side of the container. When you are marking the positive can in the blocks, scratch an X on the lid that is obvious. For the block setup, you simply put distracting odors in small tins inside the pint paint can; put the lid on the can before placing in the blocks. The pint lid should also have holes in it.

The first few times your dog smells a new odor, he may try to stop and see if he will get rewarded for it. Just keep moving and target the next block/can in the sequence. If he won't move and does a solid sit, wait him out. When he does not get rewarded he will get up and move. Don't get frustrated. The dog is trying to figure out if the rules have changed and will try some things to see if he gets rewarded for it. Nearly every dog will try something, so just work through it until you can do the exercise flawlessly with many different types of distracting odors.

He may hesitate to sniff deeply into the container; if this is the case, hold the aid in your hand and let him sniff it more toward the top

Troubleshooting

**PRO TiP**

Timing and contamination are the main things to watch here. Timing is something you and your dog will have to work out and it just takes practice. Contamination is clearly your responsibility. If you have someone to help you make up training aids and also help you lay them out, then by all means have that person handle only the distracters and be in charge of making them up. You should handle only the target odor containers.

of the can opening, and reward him when he does. Next time move the target odor tin a little deeper in the can; when he sniffs it give him the reward and lots of praise. If you use food for your reward, make it something special and different to let him know what he just did was special. Keep shaping the behavior until you get his head into the larger can as far as possible for the breed you are working with. Also, be aware that if you are working with a volatile target odor such as an accelerant material the dog may not want to get too close to sniff. In this case I believe that is a wise choice; do not worry as long as the dog will stay in the spot next to the target odor.

This is also a great drill to repeat if you are out in the real world doing searches and find your dog starts to alert on something you had not put out during training. Get some of that material and use it on the wheel to make it very clear to the dog that he should ignore that odor as it will not bring him any reward.

# PART 2: BASIC FOUNDATION DRILLS

**Notes**

# FOLLOW MY HAND DRILL

**Purpose of the Drill**

When a detector dog is doing detailed searches, it is very useful to have him following your hand so you can direct the nose to sniff in places you believe should be checked out. This drill will sharpen your dog's ability to follow your hand along any seam. It is similar to the "Aids in a Row" and "Aids in Cans" drills but a bit more elaborate in setup.

**Dog's Proficiency**

Your dog should know his odor(s) well and already be working aids in a row, cans in a row and the wheels. This drill is not for cadaver dogs searching open fields or in the water. If you have the rare cadaver dog that will be doing freight or container searches most of the time, then your dog could benefit from the exercise.

**Equipment/Training Area Needed**

Fifty to seventy-five cinder blocks. Cinder blocks should be the average 8-inch type with two holes and should be new. There are two setups for the blocks. Setup 1 is to make a long row on the ground end to end with the hole side up. Setup 2 is to build a wall such as in the photo on the next page. The blocks are set up to expose the holes on the sides and are dry stacked like a wall about six blocks high. For this drill, I find putting the smaller training aid inside a clean quart can works very well. Punch a few holes in the lid of the can. Whatever substance you are training your dog on, put that in at least six cans. Make up another 20–30 cans with distracting odors, such as candy, coffee grounds, herbs, etc. Be very careful to have one person handle the distracting odor cans and another person handle the positive training aids.

**Steps in Executing**

Cinder blocks teach the dog to follow your hand during a search. The same rules for contamination apply to cinder blocks as to anything else in detector work. You need to keep track of where you put your target odors in the cinder blocks and use only those blocks for the target odors. There can be any number of combinations for blocks. You introduce your dog to blocks just by having them in a straight row. You can have as many blocks and as long a row as you have room.

    In future sessions, you will want to change the configuration of the blocks to perhaps a circle or a line with several right-angle turns.

After a few days, you can build a cinder block wall as shown in the photo (right). The wall can hold several target odor cans in various locations throughout it, with the spaces between the positives filled with distracting odors. This creates a serpentine line for your dog to search. The purpose is to have your dog follow your hand as he sniffs each can. This exercise teaches him to trust that if he follows your hand, he will eventually find a positive odor and receive a reward.

I have found that three to four times on this drill both in the long line on the ground and on the built up wall seem to be enough for one day just to get the dog following your hand well enough.

The main trouble you will encounter here is the dog wanting to get ahead of you. This behavior is easily corrected by you spinning around and re-targeting the area where you want the dog to search. Remember when you do this to keep moving. If you are not moving fast enough, your dog will not be able to keep up a good pace that allows him to smell and move at what feels comfortable for him to process the information he is receiving. Try to be aware of your dog's pace and work to that. Don't go too fast to keep control over the search, but be aware that many people when walking backward on the search tend to slow down to almost a crawl. The flow and rhythm will come with practice.

## PRO TiP

It is easy to work the dog too much on the wall and develop timing problems. The wall is for short searches and if you do them too often or for too many repetitions, the dog will become too accustomed to short searches. So use it to develop timing and technique but then move on to real world room searches or something similar where the dog can practice the skill in a varied setting and for different durations.

## Troubleshooting

# RESPONSE IMPROVEMENT DRILL

**Purpose of the Drill**

Proofing the dog to recognize the target odor no matter how presented. You are not doing a search pattern in this exercise and should not present it as such. This is simple a drill to get a positive reaction to the target in different containers. You will build anticipation and also teach the dog to move on—that the exercise does not end with the first find.

**Dog's Proficiency**

The dog should already know the odor or odors it gets rewarded on. The response may weak. It does not matter if the dog is trained in a sit response, digging response or barking response.

**Equipment/Training Area Needed**

The best place to conduct this drill is in a small room free from drafts, noises and any other object other than the gear brought in. For this exercise, you will need to make up the following items with a target odor training aid in each:

- one small and one large cardboard box with no tape on the closure
- one small and one large cardboard box with tape on the closure
- one soft-sided suitcase
- one hard-sided piece of luggage
- one large coffee can
- one small pint metal container with a lid with five small holes punched in it
- one cosmetic container training aid

**Steps in Executing**

You will have the items listed above set up in your room in a wagon-wheel formation like the one pictured on the next page.

With the dog at your side, give the command to "find" or "seek," walk up to the dog, present the item, and allow the dog to sniff it. Reward your dog for his alert. Repeat with each item and have an assistant rotate out the items for others on the list.

Do not repeat more than two times. By then your dog's response should be sharper, as he will be anticipating the reward. Make the reward short and sweet, as you have more to do. He will learn that the game does not end at the first find. Do not rush between each

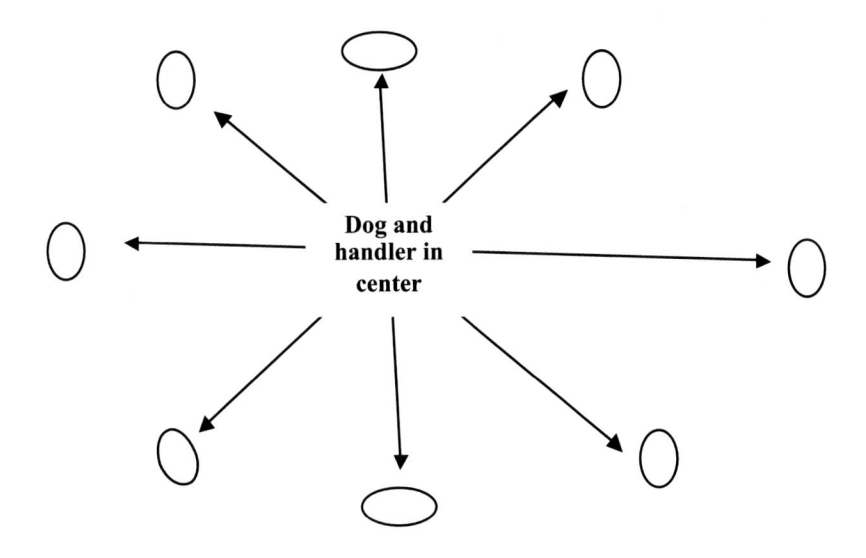

[Diagram: Dog and handler in center, with arrows radiating outward to eight surrounding items/containers arranged in a circle.]

of the items, take your time, don't stall but don't rush either. Build a little anticipation. Take a break outside the room between the first set of items and the second set.

This drill should not be used often as you can teach a false positive response if you are not careful. You are sharpening your response and should focus on that. Sit responses should be instantaneous with the first good sniff of the target odor and not before. If the dog approaches the item and sits without sniffing, you need to make sure by pointing with your hand and commanding "sniff" or whatever command you use, that he inhales first. If he still won't use his nose first, re-approach the item, making sure you are one step ahead of him and your presentation of the item is more pronounced.

If you are training using retrieve rewards, this drill works better with a mixed reward ratio. Instead of giving the towel or ball, reward at the first find with verbal and physical praise and return to the center to go on to the next item. Repeat. On the third item, give the towel or ball reward along with verbal praise. Use caution to not use the exact 3:1 for the entire session. Dogs can count, so the next time you do the set, go twice, for example, before the reward with the ball or towel, then once, then twice, then three times and so forth. Your focus should be on the dog sniffing and giving a positive response regardless of the container.

## Troubleshooting

**PRO TiP**

Do not overdo this exercise as you can train in some bad habits if done too much. Use it more for sharpening the responses. In cases where the dog appears fearful of a certain type of item, do more of the others and when the dog is jolly on those throw in the item they are fearful on, and alternate until the feared item no longer evokes any concern from the dog.

# PART III:
# ADVANCED WORK

# MAKING THE TRANSITION

Moving from the basic drills to the more advance drills will be relatively seamless providing you and your dog have learned to recognize seams and the alerts to the target odor are strong and solid. Please note, not all these drills will be relevant depending on what your dog is being trained to detect. Even if the drill is not something your dog uses in their work, there is value working a dog occasionally on something different. Dogs can get complacent just like people if they are doing the same thing repeatedly; trying something different will keep them sharp and maintain their interest.

# CASTING DRILL—OUTSIDE

**Purpose of the Drill**

The term "casting" has different meanings to different dog trainers. In this context, I am referring to the handler sending or casting the dog in a particular direction. This drill is useful for explosives, biological specimen, evidence, arson, drug, and cadaver detection dogs and the primary work area for pipeline leak detection dogs.

**Dog's Proficiency**

Your dog should have solid basic obedience and be good at following your hand and taking directions.

**Equipment/Training Area Needed**

You will need a large grassy area outside, some small metal training aids (at least a dozen) and a small shovel or garden tool for digging.

**Steps in Executing**

*Above Ground*

I have always approached this in stages to be sure the dog understands that he is going to sometimes find things on the ground proper and sometimes the source odor will come from higher up or "pooling" on the surface of the ground. At this point in the training, you probably have been working your dog outside some days, perhaps doing a row of cans or row of boxes. If you have not, then I suggest you introduce your dog to searching outside by starting with something he knows. A few repetitions of this familiar exercise outside will reduce his anxiety over what he is doing. For the next step, you can place several empty training aid containers in a row spaced about 3–4 feet apart. Now put down a container with your target odor in it and continue to make a row with additional empty containers spaced 4 feet apart. See the diagram on the next page for the layout. Since these containers are small and shallow, your dog will have to get his nose down near the ground, which is what we want. There is no need to worry about the visual cues here for now. Run him down the line using the command "seek" and reward at the appropriate container.

*Below Ground*

After you do this for 4–5 passes, put the dog away and get someone to take a spade and notch out a small divot of sod and soil just enough to put the container slightly under it. Try to keep the sod in one piece. Place each container under a divot. Make sure that the person who touches the target odor does not touch the others and vice versa. For this exercise, I like to use two other people and not touch anything myself. Once everything is in place, bring your dog back out and start the search again as before. This time you will have to target a little more closely to the divot. Do not be surprised if your dog sits the first time you do this. Chances are you stopped when you targeted it and he took your cue. Try to keep yourself moving and keep his nose on the ground. He may keep it down and then want to lift it up; just keep encouraging him to keep it down.

One thing I have used that works well is to spin around with the dog and re-target the spot if he lifts his head or gets going too fast. Your dog's nose does not need to be exactly on the ground, just close. It might take several tries before he gets the idea. On your first attempt down, you may have to pull the target odor container out a little to give him a visual cue, but after that put it back and make him work it out. As soon as you get a decent run through on this first day, stop working. Ending on a positive note is very important. Each day thereafter in training will be over larger areas and more complex, so we want to keep it simple these first few days and let the dog have many successes.

This is not complicated and should not be presented as such to the dog. The key here is to move gradually from the disturbance in the ground, being obvious to it not being so obvious. While this might not seem to exactly simulate the real world, what I have learned from countless experimentation is that the dog learns the objective better using this approach. Once he understands where he is supposed to look for the odor source in this exercise, getting him to search under real world conditions is not difficult at all. You set yourself up for failure, however, if you try to make things too complicated in this step thinking you are doing better by being more like the real world. In training we want lots of successes, and a lot of opportunities to reward the dog for a good job. I trained one dog with no more area search training than I have described here and he eventu-

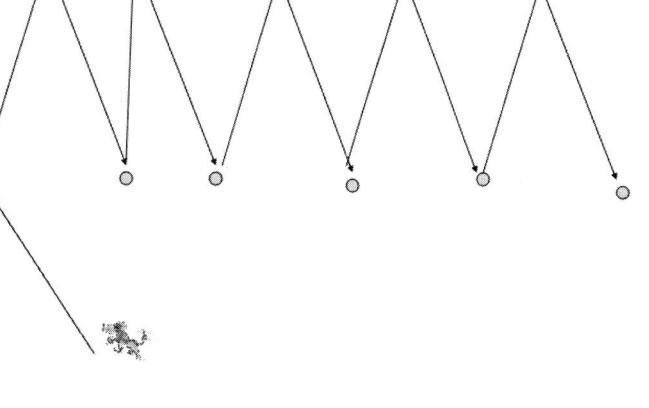

*The diagram above shows how to develop more complex patterns of searching outside above ground and teaching the zigzag pattern for covering large areas.*

ally deployed on an area search for buried weapons. He accurately located weapons in a box buried some 9 feet underground. We had never practiced on that type of situation but his schooling to look for and identify the odor in the ground using the above method gave him confidence in the real world scenario.

**Troubleshooting** If you are having trouble with the pattern, make your "targets" more obvious at first to help the dog learn and feel more comfortable with the exercise. You can make them more obvious by placing small traffic cones by each divot of sod, or use small flags. Gradually reduce the targets until the pattern is performed almost automatically by the dog. If you are working a breed of dog that has been bred for hunting, you may notice he will pick up on this pattern as it is similar to a natural quartering pattern used by hunting dogs afield. Toy dogs and smaller breeds have more trouble with the pattern but can learn it. Simply reduce the spacing to make it more their size in the beginning then gradually increase the spacing as they get more accomplished.

**Notes**

**PRO TiP**

When I teach casting drills to field retrievers, I use tables set up like a baseball diamond. While the detector dog does not need the precision casting of the field retriever to do an effective search you can use that approach to teach your dog the hand signals that go with the directions if you plan to do large areas and off-leash work.

A simple explanation with wonderful photographs of this procedure is presented in *Water Dog* by Richard A. Wolters, Dutton copyright 1964.

# BURIED DRILL FOR CADAVER DOGS

**Purpose of the Drill**  To locate buried human remains in coffins and body bags.

**Dog's Proficiency**  Recognition of human cadaver odor.

**Equipment/Training Area Needed**  Outside grassy and wooded areas, coffin, casket or body bag(s), cadaver scent. Caskets are available from a variety of sources and there are even stores that sell eco-friendly cardboard coffins. The latter are obviously less expensive and ideal for a final proofing of your dog's ability to find the cadaver odor underground. Some people argue this is a bit elaborate for practice but there is a difference in the odor dynamics when the container changes, and the more realistic the practice drill the better the performance of the dog during the real thing.

**Steps in Executing**  This part of the training is obviously limited to the cadaver dog. You can usually work out an arrangement with a local coroner to get a new body bag for training purposes. Some students have told me they found smaller bags made from the same synthetic material work great in the wheel and for area searches.

For the cadaver dog you want to be sure your dog is solid on cadaver odor on the wheel, then work the dog on the area searches explained in that section of this book. As a final step you should test the dog on the synthetic material in the scent wheel as well as buried. To test on the scent wheel, take samples of the material and place them in the blank cans of the scent wheel and then mark one piece of the same material with the cadaver scent and place it in the target odor can. Make sure you have someone else handle the target odor and piece of scented material. You want to be sure your dog is alerting on the cadaver odor and not the smell of the synthetic material of the bag. I cannot stress this enough. It is vital that you periodically test your dog to be sure he is alerting on the cadaver odor and not the synthetic material of the body bag.

A small bag is fine for burying in the training sessions since it will not have a body inside only the odor. The bag is scented with the cadaver odor then buried underground. At first, I do the searches on freshly dug "graves." To make a fresh grave, simply go out in your field area with a shovel and dig down the depth of the shovel blade. I suggest digging several holes where no cadaver scented material is placed. To begin, do not backfill the holes. Run your exercise on the holes when they are open and the scented material is in the hole but not covered. After a clean run-through with this set up, put your dog away and come back and cover up the holes, but do not tamp down the soil. Get your dog and run through all the "graves" approaching from a different direction each time but no more than four times.

If you happen to be one of the few handlers of dogs trained to find people hiding from immigration officials, you may run into a situation of a live person trying to cross the border in a coffin. I find that type of work more in the realm of protection work and training and not detector training and will not address that type of training here. For the cadaver dog, however, the coffin can present a challenge as many of the newer ones are quite airtight. Add to this 6 or 7 feet of earth to smell through and sort odor from and a dog can have a difficult time.

**PRO TiP**

Periodically test the dog on all blanks and also test for all blank material samples on the scent wheel.

## Troubleshooting

If you are getting false alerts on blank graves, your dog is probably thinking it is the disturbed earth you want him to clear on. This is a common mistake. Take you sniffer tins and go back to a straight line of just tins in an area on top of the ground first. Run the dog and reward big at the find. Then go back, without moving the tin's location, and take a divot of ground up and halfway tuck the tin in there. Repeat the search on the line several times. Next, bury the tin a little deeper. Repeat until the dog is solid on this exercise.

# BURIED DRUMS AND TANKS DRILL

**Purpose of the Drill**     The propose of this drill is to teach the dog to locate buried drums and tanks.

**Dog's Proficiency**     Your dog should have excellent search skills, strong odor recognition and very good off-leash control. This exercise is best done off leash but can be performed on a long line if the area is littered with dangers to your dog's safety and well being.

**Equipment/Training Area Needed**     Training needs to simulate the real thing so you will need a backhoe to dig up an area with large holes of various depths, some of which will have drums scented with the target odor, others will not have anything, and a few others will have clean drums.

**Steps in Executing**     Drums and tanks can be buried for a number of reasons but mostly it is done to store gasoline or toxic chemicals. Regardless of which substance you are looking for, your dog must be accurate in identifying the target odor on the wheel before you attempt to teach him to locate the substance in a sealed tank or drum beneath the ground.

There is any number of methods to teach dogs to indicate the odor of buried objects but I still prefer the sit response over the digging response even though there is no immediate danger in this type of search compared to explosives device searches. Unlike the suitcase or box search, you are not really teaching the dog to search the container. In this case you are asking them to do an area search for something buried and to identify the spot where they pick up the odor. Follow the guidelines in the drill on area searches and you should not have any difficulty in getting your dog to accurately alert to a training aid buried to 4–5 feet. When he is good on that exercise, purchase a new drum and make it up with your target odor. If it is a special chemical that you have been asked to search for, you will need to contact a chemist familiar with that substance and find out all you can about its properties. Be careful of reactions that will take place underground that might alter the original substance, create harmful gases and or start to erode the container and create a hazard. Always check with your local authorities before you attempt any type of training with any chemical substances to determine what the local, state and federal regulations and restrictions are concerning the material you are working with.

I was asked by a developer to train a dog to find buried toxic waste and found it necessary to get special permission to bury drums with the target substances even though it would be for a limited time. I also had to do the training in a secure area (one that was fenced with 6-foot barbed wire-topped chain link fencing) since I was "aging" my training drums for 6 months. The period was determined necessary to allow for chemical changes that would slightly alter the substance, and this ensured also that my dog would not be working on disturbed ground. You must always act responsibly and not contribute to further pollution of the earth. All buried material must be removed after training. All toxic material must be handled and disposed of in a safe and legal fashion.

For the training area mentioned above, I had a loader dig 20 holes deep enough to bury a 55-gallon steel drum 5 feet below the ground level. I had four positive and six negative drums and left 10 holes blank. In other words, after all the drums had been placed in 10 of the holes I had the other 10 holes filled back in and tamped just as the ones with drums had been. Six months later I came back with my dog and searched the area. I had no alerts on the disturbed earth or "blank" holes, and no difficulty with the dog locating the four positives. Careful preparations of your dog before you start searches on buried drums is something I cannot stress enough. You must be sure with lots of practice exercises that he will not give a false positive on disturbed earth. I cannot think of anything more embarrassing then to have equipment brought in at great expense and not find anything, not even an empty drum, at a place your dog indicated.

Take care of any disturbed earth false alerts using the same protocol as in the area search drill.

**PRO TiP**

Drums hold a lot of material so be sure to increase the quantity of target odor material when you are working with drums or tanks.

Troubleshooting

# BOX SHUFFLE DRILL

| | |
|---|---|
| Purpose of the Drill | This drill will slow the fast dog down, help with following the seam and eliminate false alerts on boxes. |
| Dog's Proficiency | The dog will need to have good odor recognition of the target he is trained to detect and some experience at searching boxes, containers or suitcases. |
| Equipment/Training Area Needed | For these exercises, you will need to purchase new cardboard boxes of various sizes, most of them small in the beginning. Take all normal precautions to avoid contamination with your target odors. It is best to use boxes all the same size, plain brown and new. Whoever is handling the target odors should put a sample into one of the boxes and close it by folding over and under the flaps. You should not use tape for this exercise. The handler or another clean person should assemble the empty boxes and close them in a similar manner. |
| Steps in Executing | Make a long row of the boxes and randomly place the target box in the row. Keep the boxes spaced evenly about 1–2 feet apart. Bring your dog over to first box in the row, move your hand along the "seam" formed by the two longwise flaps and command to search. Your dog should follow your hand along the seam and you should be able to see and hear him sniffing. Continue in the same manner for each box. Keep moving. Do not stop at any of the boxes. If the dog is moving too fast or not following your hand along the seam, spin around and redo that box. Reward and praise your dog when you get an alert at the positive target box. If you are using a food |

reward, be sure to have your hand on top of the box when you open it to allow your dog to eat the treats. As soon as he eats his treats take him away from the box.

The important things to focus on are the dog following the seam with his nose and the handler moving in one even fluid motion. This means that when you reach the end of the row of boxes you should not stop but keep moving away from the last box. If your dog sits then keep moving until you get to the end of the leash. Then go back and reward your dog. Taking that extra step away from the last box as if you are going to keep going will do much to instill in the dog that his job is to stop you when you pass up a container with the target odor and he can only do that by sitting. What you are teaching him is that if he sits you will come back and reward him. I have seen dogs plant themselves so solidly on a box that the handlers are nearly knocked off balance when they reach the end of the leash. That should be your goal.

As you and your dog feel more confident you can add boxes and change the configuration. The important thing is for the blank boxes at this point to contain nothing and be handled by a person who has not handled the target odor or the box with the target odor. Boxes are more difficult for dogs to search for some unknown reason, so I have learned with boxes that you need to be extremely careful about contamination issues.

You will have to be the judge of your own dog, but it would not hurt to run a dog through just this setup and no others, for 3–4

**PRO TiP**

If you are ever asked to search just one box, do not. Add more things to the search before the one box and after it. You will decrease the odds of a false sit by doing multiple items in a row.

*At left, Debby is showing students the various ways to present the boxes.*

days and a hundred or more trials before moving to the next step. The next step is to start putting distracting items—such as food, soap bars, and so on—in the other boxes and adding these to the lineup the dog is checking. When you and your dog can confidently go through 10–20 boxes with various odors flawlessly identifying the target odor, and sitting very solid, then you know you have mastered the drill.

The last step in drilling your dog is to move the boxes out of your training area and into a new environment, such as a friend's house, hotel room, office, warehouse or shopping center, bus terminal or train station. Where you move to will of course be dependent on what you are training the dog to find. Any dog used for law enforcement should be exposed to all the above-mentioned locations.

## Troubleshooting

Patience is your watchword in particular when you start this exercise. It is very helpful also to have another set of eyes watching you, as I can almost bet that you will have a tendency to stop or hesitate when you get to the end of the row of boxes, thus false cueing your dog to sit. The spotter will help to keep you honest by reminding you to keep moving. Another problem with false alerts is that certain types of adhesive tape can cause a dog to false alert depending on what your dog is trained to find.

PART 3: ADVANCED WORK 53

Notes

# FOLLOW THE SEAMS DRILL—SUITCASES

**Purpose of the Drill**  This drill is designed to get the dog to automatically recognize and search the seams of the suitcases presented to them.

**Dog's Proficiency**  Target odor recognition and how to follow your hand are the two main skills your dog should have before working on suitcases.

**Equipment/Training Area Needed**  There are hundreds of unclaimed suitcases at airports every year and it is easy to get several dozen suitcases for training from the surplus dealers that dispose of them. It is always good to have a mixture of soft-sided and hard-sided suitcases for training. Yard sales are another source for old suitcases for training. Training can be indoors or outdoors, but avoid direct hot sun and areas where exhaust fumes are prevalent.

**Steps in Executing**  Note that the target odor container is near the seam and that no adhesive type tape is being used to hold it in place. Walking backward, the handler presents the seam with the left hand, getting the dog to follow the hand along the seam. Remember to keep moving so the dog does not fake sit.

The progression in this drill is simple. You gradually close down the hard-sided suitcase until it is completely closed and the dog follows the seam of the suitcase from end to end. At this point, you introduce blank hard-sided suitcases to the lineup, constantly switching around the target odor suitcase. Keep yourself moving from one to the other. You should not stop between suitcases; think of them as one continuous seam to be searched. Do not forget to make it fun. If you and the dog are feeling good about your progress, then you can add distracting odors to the blank suitcases. I suggest really smelly things at first, such as scented soaps, strong coffee grounds, deodorant and like items.

There are three main ways to arrange the suitcases. A straight line is a good configuration to start with. It is one that evidence dogs are most likely going to use. Place the suitcases in a circle so there is no beginning or end to your pattern. In this manner, you do not have to worry about inadvertently cuing your dog by stopping at the end of the line. Finally, you can place the suitcases randomly around the edges of the room. For those training detector dogs used in law enforcement, I would also consider placing suitcases inside vehicles you are searching, inside buses and on conveyor belts.

Conveyor belts are found in such areas as airports, warehouses and shipping centers, and often cause dogs problems due to footing, noise or speed issues. If any of these points are the cause of your dog's performance problems, the best approach is to break the exercise into steps. For example, if noise is an issue work the dog in a room on an exercise he likes and at the same time have someone on the opposite side of the room move some noisy boxes, chairs or other such items to create enough of a distraction that your dog notices but not enough to scare him. Your job is to keep him working on the exercise at hand, maybe something simple like sniffing a small tin with your target odor in your hand and giving lots of praise and treats when they sniff, while the noise is going on in the background. I refer to this as proofing the dog. This proofing should continue daily as a training exercise until the dog can perform the task at hand without looking at or worrying over the noise.

If the dog is not performing well on the conveyor belt, go back to step one which is doing the search on the floor next to the conveyor belt with it turned off. Step two is working the dog on the floor next to the conveyor belt with it on. If there are no problems with that exercise, move to working the dog on top of the belt with it off. The final step is to work with the belt one, packages moving along and the dog running up and over them in a consistent fashion. Do not rush each of these steps. If you are having problems, it most likely will be from the dog being pushed too fast at any one point. I cannot recall how many problem dogs I have fixed for people just by moving back a step or two, staying there a bit longer until I see from the dog a sign that he is ready to move on. I will then do lots of short, positively reinforced sessions to let them know they made the right choice and I am happy. Problem is now fixed! Sometimes we forget some dogs just need a bit longer to get an exercise right.

All of this type of work would be in follow up to the original drill, which is to get your dog automatically searching the seams of the suitcases. As with any of these exercises, think about where you will be called out with your dog to search and try to set up training exercises to simulate these situations.

Soft-sided suitcases usually have more seams and pockets than hard-sided suitcases (this is the main difference). I try always with

**PRO TiP**

One caution: Once you have trained your dog to do the suitcase and box searches, you should never go back to searching one box or suitcase. In real life I have been called out many times to "check" out a single box with my dogs and you can believe I learned quickly how easy it is to cue a dog to a false alert with just one box around. Even if you keep yourself moving, chances are that most dogs will take a shot at getting a reward by sitting at the single box or suitcase. That habit is not one you want to instill in your dog, so just avoid it altogether in training. In the real world when you are faced with one box, look around without your dog, for other boxes you can put near the suspect box, or if that is not possible add other items to the lineup so there is more than one thing to search. Then start your search and just keep moving.

these types of suitcases to get the dog to search the seams but that may not always be possible. It is not a major issue with the soft sides if the dog does not search every seam. It is just a matter of habit you want the dog to develop more than anything else when you ask him to search every seam. You can either introduce the soft-sided luggage as a separate exercise or just mix them in with other pieces. I have not had any difficulties either way with even the fussiest of dogs.

## Troubleshooting

I have already mentioned several troubleshooting points with noise and conveyor belts. Another major issue I have seen with dogs learning to search suitcases is false alerts. Most of this stems from false cues from the handler, particularly the handler stopping and looking at the dog at the end of a row of suitcases. The dog will look back up at the handler and sit, thinking that is what is expected of him. If the handler makes the mistake and rewards the dog, a problem can start with false sitting. Simply make sure you don't stop moving until well beyond the last suitcase. If the problem is a bad one in your dog, try working in a circle for a long while until you feel the dog is pretty solid. Then go back to a line of suitcases and make sure the last one is empty for the first 10 sweeps. Also, make sure you keep moving well beyond the last suitcase in all your sweeps. On the eleventh sweep, have the last suitcase be positive to test whether the dog is really sniffing and alerting as he should.

Watch yourself as a handler that you are not cuing the dog subconsciously. If your dog misses the positive suitcase the first time, try again. If he misses it again, then go back to a simpler drill where you can watch the dog working a seam and be sure he is sniffing the entire time. Failure here is most likely due to your dog working too fast or picking up cues from the handler. If the latter, you can have a partner place blind positive suitcases out for you which should cure the problem. If the dog is working too fast, slow him down by spinning around before you get to the suitcase and making him follow your hand along the seam. If he wants to rush ahead of your hand, then spin around again and that will slow him down.

# PART 3: ADVANCED WORK

**Notes**

# FOLLOW THE SEAMS DRILL—FREIGHT

**Purpose of the Drill** — The purpose of this drill is strictly to prepare for searches on freighters or at freight terminals.

**Dog's Proficiency** — Your dog should be doing very well on boxes and suitcases before you start this work.

**Equipment/Training Area Needed** — You will need access to freight containers. Some storage yards have some to practice on, but you may have to check around to find a good source.

**Steps in Executing** — Freight containers can be made from wood or metal and are rather large. Like all other containers, you look at them from the "seam" perspective. This is precisely what you will work your dog on when searching these type of containers. I found it easiest to think of them as inside–out rooms. I start the dog in the bottom left corner and work up the seam, then come down and go across the bottom, then to the next corner seam and repeat across the bottom. If there is no alert, then I check along the top seams. I don't think there is any real value to drilling your dog too much on freight container searches. They should be practiced once or twice if you think you might be checking this type of freight. I found with my own dogs that there were only three areas where we found these containers—on trains, in ships and in some warehouses. The major problem I

**PRO TiP**
Use the pre-search technique for your freight containers to save your dog's energy.

ever encountered with freight containers was not getting the dogs to search them but rather just physically getting to the containers. Sometimes the dogs had to climb long ladder-like stairs in order to get up to where the containers were located. Ladder climbing might be something you add into your detector dog training outline as well.

The only problem I have seen with this drill is the dog handling the working surfaces where you usually find freight containers; they are often very slick. It might be a good thing to get your dog used to wearing boots so when situations come up where the surfaces are too slick or contain contaminants your partner will be protected.

## Troubleshooting

# FOLLOW THE SEAM DRILL—VEHICLES

**Purpose of the Drill**

When conducting a vehicle search, the main objective is to check all the seams of the vehicle where odor may leak out from the inside and to check any other areas on the outside where something may be concealed. There is no real right or wrong way to do the vehicle search but experience dictates that you need to be consistent in your searches and you should be efficient so as to minimize the dog's efforts. It is for these reasons that a systematic approach is taken to vehicle searches. The systematic approach will also help you keep straight which parts have been searched, and it just looks more professional when you have a method for searching the car.

There are three classes of vehicles for our purposes here, the automobile, the truck and the bus. When your dog learns the bus search pattern, you will see how this pattern will transfer to airplanes and passenger trains. Each class of vehicle has its own unique set of search parameters that a dog needs to master, and each will be discussed separately in this chapter.

**Dog's Proficiency**

Your dog will need to be competent on following your hand and recognizing seams.

**Equipment/Training Area Needed**

The first consideration when training a dog to do vehicle searches is a source of vehicles. County or state impound lots are perfect if you have access to them. You need to expose your dog to a variety of shapes, sizes and makes of cars in order for him to become proficient. For the first few days, four or five vehicles—perhaps those parked in your yard or neighborhood—will do. Mark your training logbook carefully so you will be able to identify where you put what on which vehicle. This is very important in terms of contamination. You can only use a vehicle so much before the odors start to contaminate it.

**Steps in Executing**

*Automobile*

From the detector dog trainer's perspective, cars are either new (made after 1999) or old (made before 1998) with the main differences being in the ventilation system of the vehicle and the "air tightness" of the interior. Otherwise, the search of all vehicles is conducted in the same manner. I will go over the procedure for conducting a vehicle first so that you will have in mind the goal you are working toward in the initial training. The training is done in steps to help your dog feel more comfortable working around a vehicle first of all and to condition him to look in all the proper spots on the vehicle second of all.

When conducting a vehicle search, there is always a pre-search sweep made around the vehicle. This is simply walking around the vehicle with a loose leash allowing the dog to sniff casually at the vehicle. The pre-search is done for several reasons. First, it allows your dog to warm up, get a sense of the area and smells associated with it; in many cases you will get an alert from the dog. Even though an alert is given during the pre-search a more detailed search is conducted all the same. The pre-search is started at the right front bumper of the vehicle. When you reach the left front bumper, you immediately begin the detailed search. The detailed search is a matter of checking the seams of the vehicle carefully from one end to the other. You begin with the grill and hood, move to the first wheel well, then the door seams, the gas cap, the second wheel well, the rear bumper, trunk, third wheel well, door seams, fourth wheel well, and finally end up where you began. A well trained team will rarely take longer then 3–4 minutes to clear one vehicle when the searches are conducted in this manner.

When conducting the search of any vehicle, you begin on the left side of the front bumper. Your first concern is to search the lower part of the bumper from one end to the other. Think of it as a large seam. If you are able to get your dog to search low and keep his head under the bumper, he will get any odor coming from the engine area. To train the dog in this behavior, simply put the training aids with the target odor under the bumper. Some makes of cars have open bumpers where there is a handy ledge very well suited for this purpose. These are the best cars to start with, but that may not be a luxury you have. If you can only get access to new

*For the drill, you will focus on the seams—arrows show the direction your hand should be going, starting from below the passenger-side front bumper.*

cars with tightly molded bumpers, you may have to be creative in coming up with ways to place your training aid. Avoid using tape if at all possible. The principle behind this step is the same as for the previous step: You are conditioning your dog to search the bumper and grill in a systematic manner, so set your two aids up along the bottom spaced enough apart that the dog can sniff along the bumper edge a little before he comes to another aid. Practice until your dog is going from end to end keeping his head down under the bumper the whole time. When the dog has mastered this step, you can start hiding your target odor aids in the grill. You will bring the dog along the bottom first, going from left to right and then turn around and start the whole move over again, only this time have him search the grill area above from left to right. The handler moves ahead of the dog using a sweeping motion of the hand along the "seam" that he wants the dog to follow. It might seem a little awkward at first but it gets easier as you practice. Since there is no grill in the back of the vehicle, you search the bumper below only and then the trunk seam instead of the grill. When your dog has mastered these two areas, you can combine them with the wheel wells, always going in order from front left around the car and back again to the front left where you end.

### Doors

The final stage of vehicle search training is teaching your dog to search the seams of doors. It is nearly impossible to get a training aid in the door seam so this is where a person needs to be a little creative. If you have access to an old junk car you can have your way with, you can make holes in the frame of the door that will allow the dog to get used to the idea of searching the seams of doors. If you only have new cars that cannot be damaged, you can try repackaging the target odor into a container that will fit in the crack of the doors. It will actually help your dog to visualize the seam of the door better if it is cracked. You should introduce the dog to the door seams the same as you did to the wheel well. Begin by just walking him up to the door, use you hand to get him to search along the bottom seam first and the side seam up as far as his nose can reach while his feet are on the ground, and repeat this with each door. After several tries, your dog should have the idea of what you want him to do. Now you are ready to put it all together and begin to do a proper vehicle search from start to finish.

## The Complete Vehicle Search Sequence

The first time you do this search, use new vehicles that your dog has not searched before. I generally use two or three target odor aids for the first search. I like to place one low in one of the bumpers, one in the seam of a door and one in a wheel area. You begin with the pre-search, which is conducted on a loose leash held in the left hand, and with the handler facing the dog and walking backward. Using her right hand, the handler motions toward the car the whole time, and will give one or two search commands. The pace on the pre-search is brisk—you are not running but moving out so the dog is trotting.

As soon as you get to the starting point again, which is always the right front bumper, you begin by moving your hand along the bottom of the bumper and commanding the dog to search. When you get to the end of the bumper you turn around and go back to the beginning and search along the grill. When you get to the end of the grill, you move directly to the first wheel well. From there you go to the door seam, the second wheel well area and then move on to the rear bumper. Go the full length of the rear bumper before you turn around and make the dog search the trunk seam. When you are finished with that area, move to the next wheel well area, door seams and the final wheel well area.

I have not mentioned gasoline openings previously but they are also an area you want to teach your dog to search. I prefer to teach this last, after the full search pattern is beginning to feel more comfortable to both my students and their dogs. Use your judgment as to where you want to introduce this area to your dog in training. There is no right or wrong here; wherever you think it fits in, you should introduce it. Teach it as a separate point, however you decide to do it.

## Trucks

There are many different kinds of trucks, and each type presents a different set of problems for the detector dog. Before you move on to trucks, you and your dog should feel comfortable with the automobile search. Your dog will have a good idea of how to keep his head low on the pre-search to find any odor that has dropped below the vehicle and to search all the seams he sees on his second pass around. Conducting a search of a smaller truck is no different than

**PRO TiP**

If you have a large number of vehicles to search, work your dog off leash and do a sweep around the vehicles looking for a change of behavior first. When you see any change, do the detailed search only on that vehicle. This procedure will save your dog's energy and allow you to search more vehicles.

conducting a search of an automobile except that trucks without a cap over the truck bed do not have to have the trunk, or in this case the tailgate seam, searched. You simply move the dog around the truck's rear bumper keeping his head low and underneath.

If the truck is a service type truck with toolbox compartments, you will need to search the boxes along the seams. Panel vans and larger trucks require a bit more work on the part of the dog who must reach up to smell the grill area and door seams. What is different for the dog and handler is that tractor trailers are very tall, in dog terms, and very long. There are usually wheel wells only in the front part of the truck and not in the back, however, the back wheels usually have on the back side some area that you can direct your dog to search. When I first start my dog searching tractor trailers, I like to hide at least one training aid in the back of the trailer tires. I hide the remainder of the target odor training aids on the underside of the trailer or along the inside of the trailer door by the seam where the doors meet the floor of the trailer. Trailers are tall enough that as you go around them the dog can keep four feet on the ground, just lift his head and sniff the air along the floor of the trailer. Remember, when your dog alerts your food reward should always come from the source of the odor to the dog. When you reward like this, particularly on trailer searches, you will soon condition your dog to look up and sniff rather then keep his head along the ground.

### Bus—Outside Search

Buses are not that much different to search than cars or trucks, except you have more room to move around once you get inside. As with other vehicle searches, we begin with the left front bumper area and work around the bus in a counterclockwise direction until you get to the starting point again. The difference between a bus and other vehicles is in the seams and doors. The bus has very little on the outside for the dog to check except the under carriage, so concentrate on getting your dog to look and sniff that area. There is on most buses a paneled side area in the rear that has either a grate or hatch-like door cover. This should be searched by having your dog follow the seams. The same is true for the rear escape door, except due the height the dog can only check the bottom seam of the door. On commercial buses, there will be cargo storage areas all around the bottom of the bus and each of these are searched in a similar manner.

*Inside the bus a dog may not be able to get between the seats but should be sniffing below them and zigzagging while working the aisle.*

## Bus—Inside Search

You can think of this drill much the same way as an area search only in a smaller space. The inside of the bus contains seats in various arrangements and maybe a toilet facility, so the search is quick and easy. The side-to-side pattern is shown in the photograph on the next page. Since the bus is a closed area, odor will accumulate and concentrate. Don't be surprised if there is a target odor present in the bus such that as soon as your dog enters the bus you get a strong change of behavior from him. In most cases the dog will go directly to the source.

## Troubleshooting

Since this drill is approached in steps, you can use the steps to help with troubleshooting. Simply move back one step from where you are having problems and work that step a few more times before moving on. You can also make the target more apparent at the point where the dog is not searching so well. I don't suggest you do that too much, however, as your dog will get lazy and start to look for cues and clues from you. If you are having real difficulty keeping the dog on the vehicle and following the seams, go back to the seam wall drill until you can do it perfectly, quickly and in one fluid motion.

# ROOM SEARCH DRILL

**Purpose of the Drill**

Your dog is already used to working inside at this point so the transitions to interior room searches should not be too difficult. Below, I outline the procedure for an explosive dog's search and speak to the exceptions. Termite detectors will be looking at walls and floors only and drug dogs usually will not check the door before entering, nor will the cadaver dog. I suggest you do check it though with your drug dog if it is of hollow-core construction. Arson dogs have varying amounts of walls and furniture to check and it is usually a mess. The best I have found is to train them in a cluttered non-burnt room just to get them used to the exercise of searching and then when a fire scene is available use it after it has been cleared. Depending on what you find on a fire scene and the hazards around, you just have to organize your search as best you can.

**Dog's Proficiency**

The dog must know his odors well enough that there is no hesitation in the alerts and they are strong alerts where the dog stays with the odor.

**Equipment/Training Area Needed**

Small training aids, a room with furniture, or a small warehouse section with varying types of containers and stored freight.

**Steps in Executing**

The detailed room search is no different than the other searches in that you should think of it as checking any and all seams. You will also be checking selected targets, such as outlet boxes, switches and trash cans. If a wall contains a closed closet door, have your dog smell along the bottom seam. The search goes from the outside edges of the room toward the inside, left to right. You search low then high.

To begin teaching the room search, use a room with little or no furniture. The new thing you are teaching the dog in this search is to look in walls for the target. By now your dog should follow your hand with his nose when you command seeks. If your dog shows any sign of not being able to handle a detailed room search, you will need to go back and practice having the dog follow your hand as you target where you want him to sniff.

To begin the detailed, search start at the left of the door, turn around and walk backward, leash in your left hand and your right hand sweeping along the part of the room where the wall meets the floor. Command "seek" once and commence going around the room, staying close to the wall. Continue until you come to an electrical outlet. Tap the outlet and repeat "seek." Then continue with your dog as before, tapping every outlet as you pass it. Do not stop at the outlet; target it and keep moving. Here's the tricky part for the handler: You need to keep moving but you don't want to move so fast that your dog starts to miss your targeting cues. It takes practice to get this down smoothly so just be patient while you both learn. You will want to have some target odor in the wall sockets every so often so your dog will begin to learn to target them himself.

I have found it useful when teaching the detailed search to put some aids behind the baseboard also. This way, for the first few times around the room the dog gets the idea to check the outlets and also keep his nose near the floor as the nose will most likely yield finds, hence food. For the first few training exercises, eliminate furniture from the room where possible so the searches go quickly. You should be able to repeat the detailed room search five times. After that the dogs will remember where all the aids are and will not search any longer; they will just run to the next aid and sit. The next day do your search in a different room. I found unused schoolrooms excellent for this training. The majority of dogs will do the

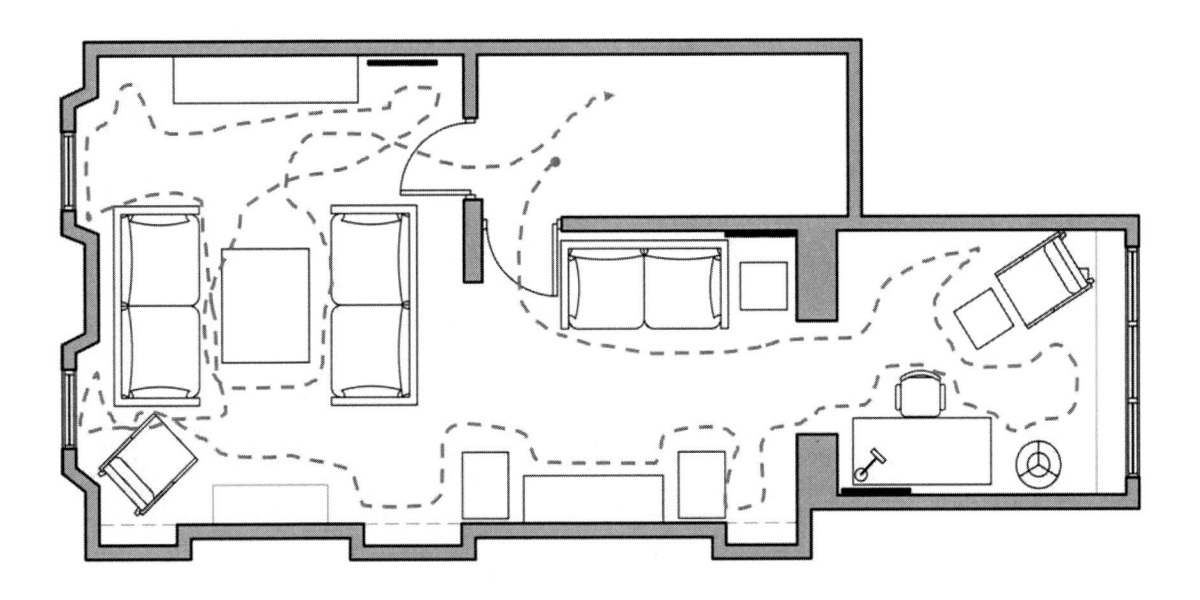

> **PRO TIP**
>
> Remember the following pattern for searches:
> - Left to right
> - Outside to inside
> - Low to high

detailed exterior wall search well after two days, including checking any closet door seams.

By day three, you can add the "high" search points, which are the window ledges and the light switch plate covers. Most rooms have a light switch near the door. So let's say you come in the room and start your search to the left but you notice the switch. Have the dog check the low point first but before moving on command "Hup" and point to the switch by lightly tapping it, then tell him "seek." Do not linger here; as soon as the dog sniffs the switch move on with the rest of the room search. When you go to the window, have him check the bottom seam only. If you come across a long window during your search, do the baseboard below the window first when you get to it, then swing around and go a second time through the area but targeting the window on this pass.

When you finally introduce furniture into the room, the search pattern will change slightly. You will do your pre-search the same way but on the detailed search, you will look for "seams" in the furniture to target for your dog. For example, a drawer will create a seam where it fits in its place, just as a cushion will on an upholstered chair. The key point is to be fluid in your search. Keep moving and leave it to the dog to alert you—by solid planted sits—that he has sniffed the target odor. If you are a very observant handler you will begin to see the change in behavior of the dog as he gets a sniff of something even before he sits. As I said earlier, you will know when you do the pre-search whether or not the room contains something positive.

I continue to do room searches in various locations for 14 days of training before I feel I can now have 1) fewer aids planted with the dog still targeting the critical spots and 2) have blank rooms. A borrowed house or unused schoolhouse is great for this stage of training. You will need to set out maybe two target odors out of five rooms. Do not do this too often though. You should periodically do it for the remainder of the training period. There needs to be variation in the amount of time the dog searches before he finds the training aid but you also have to balance out what I call the boredom factor. Dogs get bored easy and it will turn off a good dog if you try to repeat things too often.

When you get out in the real world doing real searches in buildings and houses, you will carry a "plant" with you. After you clear an area, have someone place this down and go back through that area with the dog to allow him the chance for a reward and to keep his interest up. This is not necessary for training exercises, since you will have multiple "plants" in place.

## Troubleshooting

If you have laid a solid foundation for your dog, you should not have any problems with executing these drills. The biggest problem is to keep the dog focused during the searches. By carrying a small positive sniffer with you and once in a while having someone "plant" it in an area you have already searched, your dog should remain alert.

# FOLLOW THE SEAM DRILL—WINDOWS

| | |
|---|---|
| Purpose of the Drill | The purpose of this drill is to get the dog to completely search a window. |
| Dog's Poficiency | Prior to working on windows your dog should have good skills on the seam wall. |
| Equipment/Training Area Needed | A room with a lot of individual windows is the best training area. |
| Steps in Executing | When you go to the window, have your dog check the bottom seam, or if there is a ledge, along there only. If there is a long window to search, when you get to it do the baseboard below the window first then swing around and go a second time through the area but target the window on this pass. Look at the diagram below to see the pattern. Your dog can only go as far as he can reach standing on his hind legs so do not worry about him not being able to reach all the way to the top. After you have practiced windows enough that you feel he can handle the search well, you may want to place a positive training aid at the top of the window and test whether he can or will find it. |
| Troubleshooting | If your dog does not alert on the training aid at the top of the window, try moving it down along the side but high up. If he still does not alert, move it down the side further until you get an alert. Do this when the dog is not present and cannot see you placing the aid. Windows are easiest to teach to explosives dogs because we use the explosive detonation cord in short pieces for the positive aid. For other substances like termites, this will be more difficult and may require some creative thinking to make it a fair test. |

# PART 3: ADVANCED WORK

**Notes**

**PRO TiP**

Windows are difficult and boring at the same time for the dog as they are working a lot on two legs. Try to keep this exercise short and under four runthroughs in one room.

# FOLLOW THE SEAM DRILL—DOORS

**Purpose of the Drill** — This drill will help your dog learn to recognize and search the seams around doors as well as practice jumping up on a flat surface to search.

**Dog's Proficiency** — Your dog should be following your hand very well and be capable of doing room searches.

**Equipment/Training Area Needed** — A seam wall. The seam wall is piece of plywood with slits at different heights and in different orientations that has places on the back side to hold the training aids in place.

**Steps in Executing** — To teach the dogs to perform the door search or to perfect their skills at it, I suggest you use what I refer to as a seam wall. This is nothing more than a sheet of plywood with grooves in various lines on a frame to keep it upright. The back sides of the grooves have slots for holding small training aids. The seams on the wall are more obvious than on a door and thus it is used to further perfect the exercise of your dog following your hand during a search.

You approach this wall just as you did the pallets or the cinder block wall. Take your dog up to the wall and give your command to "find it" as you move your hand along the seam. You will need

*A seam wall should have vertical and horizontal seams of differing widths.*

to keep the leash short at first to help guide the dog until he is used to doing the search. Keep your hand moving from the beginning to the end until the dog sits and alerts when he reaches the positive aid.

The vertical seam is going to be taller than what your dog has experienced in the pallet setup. Bring him to the seam starting at the bottom and command him to find it while moving your hand upward along the seam. As you get to the point where the dog can no longer reach your hand, command him to "hup." This is an old British training term that is a contraction of "High up." I like it because it is unique and is saved for only detector work, and is not confused with other words in the dog's mind. It might take a bit of work to get your dog to jump up on his hind feet and continue sniffing, but with patience on your part he will get it soon enough. The first time he does, be sure to lavish on the praise and give an extra big reward. If you have a lot of trouble getting the dog to jump up, move the positive aid down to the spot just above where he can reach with four feet on the ground. Encourage the dog to jump just a little to get his nose on the aid. When you reward him be sure he sees the food in your hand coming from the location of the training aid. This point is important. The reward should always come from the source of the odor.

*Left: Place aids on the seam higher than the dog can reach.*

When you perfect the technique on the seam wall, try out a few doors. Start with solid doors first and make sure you dog is comfortable on them before you introduce him to glass doors.

When you are on a real world search of a building, searching the door is always going to be your first step depending on the type of search you are doing. The procedure is simple and shown in the diagram at left. Start with your hand at the bottom of the door seam and command "seek." As you do this you start to move your hand along the seam toward the top of the seam. Your dog's nose

*A typical door search goes from left to right, checking the seams on the sides and the bottom. Keep your dog's nose on the seams.*

*Double doors are searched using the same basic pattern as for single doors.*

should be following your hand. He may on the first go around try to alert before reaching the source. If he does, verbally say "good dog" but do not reward him with food. Rather, get him back up on the door seam and closer to the source. As soon as he reaches the source, if he doesn't immediately on his own try to sit, command "sit." To reward him, put your hand with the food on the source and bring it down to the dog. He cannot sit any closer to the source obviously, but he still sees the food coming from the source. If you get lazy and do not follow this pattern, in short order your dog will refuse to jump up and check high seams.

Troubleshooting

If you run into any problems here, it will be with the dog not jumping up to search as high as he can reach or he won't keep his nose to the seam. If he is reluctant to search high, be sure he is not in some physical pain; otherwise this will have to be a search where the reward is of a higher value than the others. Be careful though not to always make the high part of the search be the positive find; vary it enough to keep him on his toes and honest.

**Notes**

**PRO TiP**

In the real world many things are found in and around the doors of buildings so always plan in training situations to have the doors periodically loaded with your target odor if that is appropriate for the type of searches you are doing.

# PART IV:
# PRACTICAL MATTERS

## SAFETY AND FIRST AID

Safety is something we all know about but few really take the time to learn or practice. When an emergency hits, panic suddenly sets in and for one out of four instances, a life is lost because the person did not know the right thing to do to save a dog's life. Our dogs are exposed to dangers all the time and rely on us to keep them safe. Detector dogs are exposed more than the average dog to many insidious and other dangers and need us as their partners to be prepared.

I have included this section to raise awareness to the safety factor when working your detector dog but in no way profess it is complete or the only thing you will need. I strongly urge you to take a pet safety, first aid and CPR class. The premier school for this is Pet Tech™ and on their website you can find a local certified instructor and course. They also offer an excellent application for your iPhone, iPad or Android that is comprehensive and includes everything you need during an emergency right there at your fingertips. More information on how to download this is in the resources section of this book. You should always have a safety first aid kit for your dog with you when you are out working. When you take the first aid course, you will be taught what to have in the kit and how to use it to stabilize your dog before transporting to the nearest vet.

The primary dangers to detector dogs fall into five broad categories. Be aware of these dangers in every situation you put your dog into before you begin working. It is a habit that will keep you and your dog safe while working.

## Cuts and Bleeding

In the course of my career while out in the fields and around buildings working dogs, I cannot remember how much broken glass and other sharp metal edges I have seen. Barbed wire fence pieces left on the ground are another danger to tender paw pads when working fields and open areas in the country. Aside from all this there is also the real danger of your dog being attacked by another dog, or you could end up in a car accident, where your dog could be cut and bleeding.

## Insects and Parasites

Poisonous insect bites and parasites are often something we do not notice immediately but the effect on the dogs can be at worst crippling or lethal. When I teach classes to professional detector handlers, there is always a 30-minute session at the end of the training day for grooming and examination of the dog from eyes and ears all the way to the tip of the tail, topside and bottom side as well. Once you get in the regular habit of doing this, you are more likely to notice the slightest change or find that pesky disease-carrying tick before it becomes embedded and infects your dog.

## Heat Stroke and Hyperthermia

I remember early on as a young instructor learning one day of a military dog who was left in a car with the window rolled up and the air conditioner running. The handler left to do something thinking all was well and fine on this hot summer day for his dog in the car. The car stalled out and the AC of course stopped. Within minutes the dog's brain was literally boiling. I have seen hunters run dogs so hard in the heat that the dogs dropped from heat stroke as they could not cool off quickly enough. Always be aware of the fact that dogs cannot regulate their temperatures as well or as quickly as people. Often a dog's love and desire to do what you have asked them to do will overrule their good sense to stop before they overheat. Look for heavy labored breathing and excessive panting as two of the signs of overheating. If you note the slightest loss of coordination in your dog's work, stop the work immediately. Make sure you always have fresh cool water for your dog during your searches and working sessions, winter and summer.

Depending on the breed of dog you use, excessive chilling can be as much of a problem as overheating. I recall working my dogs in Minnesota in 26°F below zero weather and learning that paw pads can get frostbite, too. Northern breeds have extra circulatory structure to accommodate the cold but even those breeds need boots when the temperatures dip too low below zero. Another hazard in cold weather for a dog is chemicals used to keep streets, parking lots and sidewalks clear of ice and snow. Many handlers are carrying boots for winter work. This is a great idea; just be sure to train your dog to wear them before you need him to wear them.

## Poisons

The Pet Tech™ application (see page 71) includes a complete listing of known poisons to dogs. The application also shows you exactly what to do if your dog should ingest a poison. You can't be too careful when doing searches with your dog and you really need to do a "pre-search" of the area where you will be working your dog before you bring him in to identify, and if possible remove, any hazards. So many homes, warehouses, offices and even storage buildings have multiple chemicals, like turpentine, herbicides, deodorizers, disinfectants, rat poison and other things which could do serious damage to your dog.

The main things to remember with poisoning are to keep your cool; identify, or better still, collect a sample of what you think the poison is; if your dog starts to vomit collect a sample of that for the vet; call the vet to let them know you are coming; and transport your dog immediately.

## Choking

Dogs love to put things in their mouths and that makes choking a potential emergency you will have to deal with. Your pet safety class will teach you the ways to deal with choking in a dog but I think the best course here is a twofold approach. First, train your dog to do a perfect and prompt "Leave It" when you command. It is one of those things you can teach your dog easily and it will save his life when you need to use it. The second part of my approach is the same for poisons. When you take a dog out to work in an area, always pre-search the area where you will be working your dog before you bring him in to identify—and if possible, remove—any hazards. I can't say this enough: Please make it your habit. There are so many instances of dogs getting hurt and even dying due to the handler not taking the time to look out for her partner.

These are just a few of the hazards that can potentially affect your canine partners. If you have spent the time training your dog to be a great detector, take just a little more time and learn the basics of how to keep him safe and what to do during an emergency by taking an accredited Pet Tech™ safety course, keeping a first aid kit with your dog gear, and having the Pet Tech™ application on your iPhone.

PART 3: ADVANCED WORK   81

Notes

# APPENDIX

# RESOURCES

To buy the First Aid application for your iPhone, go to the iTunes store and under the Health tab look for Pet Tech™ pet safety and first aid. When prompted use reference code DK1621. The application is $4.99.

To find a Pet Tech™ instructor, go to www.pettech.com

To order tins for training, visit www.chilbrook.com/store.html

Pint and gallon paint cans in small quantities, can be purchased at your local home improvement store.

Pseudo Cadaver Scents can be purchased through Sigma Chemicals Sigma. Pseudo is a trademark of Sigma-Aldrich Biotechnology LP and Sigma-Aldrich Co.

http://www.sigmaaldrich.com/catalog/ProductDetail.do?lang=en&N4=P4304|FLUKA&N5=SEARCH_CONCAT_PNO|BRAND_KEY&F=SPEC

## ABOUT THE AUTHOR

Debby Kay was one of the early trainers of search and rescue dogs in North America; as an outgrowth of her volunteer work, she eventually left her position as a research scientist with the Federal Government to become the training director of International Detector Dogs Ltd. In this capacity, she trained the first toxic waste detection dog and was an early pioneer of using dogs to help ecologists, geologists and field biologists find targeted specimens for their research.

She has taught classes for dog professionals and amateurs alike all over the world. As a contractor, Debby trained some of the first classes of dogs and instructors for the fledgling ATF explosive dog program in Front Royal, Virginia.

She has been breeding dogs under the Chilbrook prefix since 1969, including Labrador Retrievers, Golden Retrievers, German Shepherds, Belgium Malinois, Belgium Sheepdogs, Australian Shepherds, Border Collies, German Shorthair Pointers, English

Cocker Spaniels, Bloodhounds, Bluetick Coonhounds, Foxhounds, Beagles, and Chihuahuas. Dogs from her program have earned over 300 titles in the field, and in conformation, tracking, agility and obedience rings. In addition, hundreds of her dogs work as service dogs for the blind and physically disabled, seizure alert dogs, and assistance dogs for the autistic. They also serve as working members of police, security, and search and rescue organizations around the world.

Debby is an all breed conformation judge and hunt test judge. She is the author of the *Labrador Breeder's Handbook*, and conducts seminars nationally on Labrador Retrievers, Super Sniffer™ workshops for detector dog training, and Pet Safety and First Aid, as well as teaching her unique dynamic living concepts on human/animal partners. She lives with her husband, Sam Cochran, on their farm in Harpers Ferry, West Virginia.

# Notes

# INDEX

Page numbers in bold indicate illustrations.

accelerant detection, 14, 34
adhesive tape, 52
aids in a can drill, 26–27
aids in a row drill, 24–25
*Animals in Translation* (Grandin), 19
arson dogs, 42, 66
automobiles, 60–63, **61**. See also vehicles

behavior, shaping, 16–17, 18
biological specimen dogs, 42
black powder, smokeless, 14
bleeding and cuts, 78
body bags, 46–47
body language, 18
box shuffle drill, 50–52
boxes, 50–52, **50**, **51**, 55
buried drill for cadaver dogs, 46–47
buried drums and tanks drill, 48–49
buses, 64–65, **65**. See also vehicles

cadaver dogs, 42, 46–47, 66
cadaver odors, 46–47
cans, 26–27, 27, 28, 30, 32–34, 36
cars, 60–63, **61**. See also vehicles

caskets, 46–47
casting drill, 42–44
chilling, 79
choking, 80
cinder blocks, 32, 33, 36–37
clicker training, 16–17
coffins, 46–47
containers, freight, 58
contamination, 34
conveyor belts, 55
cuts and bleeding, 78

detailed searches, 61, 64
distracting odors, 33, 36, 37, 52
doors, 72–74, **72–74**
drills
    aids in a can, 26–27
    aids in a row, 24–25
    box shuffle, 50–52
    buried drill for cadaver dogs, 46–47
    buried drums and tanks, 48–49
    casting, 42–44
    follow my hand, 36–37
    follow the seam drill, doors, 72–74, **72–74**
    follow the seam drill, vehicles, 60–65
    follow the seam drill, windows, 70, **70**
    follow the seams drill, freight, 58
    follow the seams drill, suitcases, 54–56
    odor discrimination, 32–34
    response improvement, 38–39, **39**
    room search, 66–69, 67
    training wheel, 28–31
drug dogs, 42, 66
drums, 48–49, **48**

evidence dogs, 42
explosive detection, 14, 42

false alerts, 28, 47, 49, 52, 55, 56
field retrievers, 44

"find it" command, 18
fire scenes, 66
first aid, 77–80
follow my hand drill, 36–37
follow the seam drill, doors, 72–74, **72–74**
follow the seam drill, vehicles, 60–65
follow the seam drill, windows, 70, 70
follow the seams drill, freight, 58
follow the seams drill, suitcases, 54–56
freight containers, 58

gas, natural, 14
gasoline, 14
Grandin, Temple, 19
graves, 47

heat stroke, 78–79
hyperthermia, 78–79
hypothermia, 79

insects, 78

Jenny (dog), 19

"leave it" command, 80

marijuana, 14
mercaptoacetic acid, 14

narcotic detection, 14
natural gas, 14

odor discrimination drill, 32–34
outside searching, 42–44, **43**

pace and pacing, 15, 37
parasites, 78
patterns, search, 68
Pet Tech™, 77, 80
poisons, 79–80

pre-searches, 58, 61, 63

response improvement drill, 38–39, **39**
retrievers, field, 44
room search drill, 66–69, **67**

safety, 77–80
seam wall, 72, 72
seams
doors, 72–74, **72–74**
freight containers, 58
suitcases, 54–56
vehicles, 60–65
windows, 70, **70**
search patterns, 68
shaping behavior, 16–17, 18
sniffer tins, **14**, 24–25
stress, 18–19
suitcases, 54–56, **54**

tanks, 48–49, **48**
tape, adhesive, 52
target odors, 13–20, **17**
termite detectors, 66
tins, **14**, 24–25
toxic materials, 49
tractor trailers, 64. See also vehicles
training wheel drill, 28–31, **29**, **30**
trucks, 63–64. See also vehicles

vans, 64. See also vehicles
vehicles, 60–65, **61**
Volhard, Jack & Wendy, 18

walls, 36–37, **37**, 66–68, 72, **72**
Water Dog (Wolters), 44
weapons, 44
wheels, 28–31, **29**, 32–34
Whitney, Leon, 17
windows, 70, **70**

Wolters, Richard A., 44

zigzag patterns, **43**